About the Author

Jim Maxwell is the most experienced cricket
commentator on the ABC radio team. He has
worked on over 140 Tests, including four tours to
the West Indies, three to India and Pakistan,
and three World Cups since joining the ABC
as a trainee in 1973.

Jim also edits the ABC Cricket Book, Australia's longest-
running cricket publication.

The title "Stumps" is not intended to be valedictory; just
a pause for reflection at the end of another day's play.

JIM MAXWELL
STUMPS

To Madonna, Hamish and Oliver

Author: Jim Maxwell
Managing Editor: Philip Gore
Designer: Vanessa Holden/ad+d
Art production: Juliana Tufegdzic
Photography: allsport
Additional photography: Jim Maxwell
Marketing Director: Stephen Balme

Published jointly by Hardie Grant and
Media21 Publishing Pty Ltd
© Media21 Publishing 2001
© Jim Maxwell

Hardie Grant
12 Claremont Street, South Yarra, Victoria 3141
Ph: (03) 9827 8377 Fax (03) 9827 8766
Email: juliepinkham@hardiegrant.com.au

Media21 Publishing Pty Ltd
30 Bay Street, Double Bay, NSW 2028
Ph: (02) 9362 1800 Fax (02) 9362 9500
Email: m21@media21.com.au

Printed by Griffin Press

The National Library of Australia
Cataloguing-in-Publication

Maxwell, Jim.
Stumps: the way I see it

ISBN 1 74064 038 1.
1. Test matches (Cricket) - Australia. 2. Test matches
(Cricket) - England. 3. Test matches (Cricket) - India.
I. Title.
796.35865

JIM MAXWELL
STUMPS
The Way I See It

Acknowledgments

To Glenn Mitchell, whose diary-of the Indian
tour was invaluable and covered the gaps in
my fading memory.
To Philip Gore and Stephen Balme, who gently
guided and elicited the good oil, and rewrote
the rest of it on the other side of lunch.
To my mother for all that typing,
and to Tim Cohen and Jerry Thiedeman for many
wonderful days playing cricket.
To the listeners for listening, and to the ABC,
particularly the late Bernard Kerr,
Derek White, and Peter Longman for
giving me the opportunity to prattle on from
the commentary box.

CONTENTS

Introduction

No cricketing year is without its
memorable events, on-field and off.
For Australia, the achievements of
2000–2001 may never be surpassed. They
will not be forgotten by those of us who
were privileged to share them.

Cricket is slow, thank God for that, when fever drives
 the mind
Through burning miles we leave more miles behind,
To build new hells and let the beauty go.
Let's hold this picture, though the seasons pass –
The sunlit field, the shadows on the grass,
 And keep it slow,
With brief swift moods – the catch, the stolen run –
The whole tranquil pageant in the sun,
A gracious game, with fickle ebb and flow,
That breeds good fellows, kind and quiet-faced,
Not bound upon the chariot wheels of haste.

 from *Punch*

The author at his post in the ABC commentary position during the tour of India. Technical problems were always "waiting for the man" to fix, and picking up the phone was sometimes the only way to get the live coverage through to Australia.

This nostalgic, gentle appreciation of cricket reflects a mood, a pace that we can still relate to, but its sentiment reads anachronistically to a generation brought up on instant information and indulgence.

Australia plays cricket like Tiger Woods hits a golf ball. There's an explosion of power, of aggression, and a control, a discipline that buries the ball in the cup, or in the safe hands of Mark Waugh at slip.

Australians are enjoying an epoch of sporting excellence, particularly the achievements of their cricket team, who keep winning stylishly. Many moments linger pulsatingly. Most of them occurred in India.

Adam Gilchrist's high-risk attack on Australia's subsequent nemesis, Harbhajan Singh, in Mumbai's Wankhede Stadium, stands out as a thrilling demonstration of skill and audacity. Hitting against the spin Gilchrist on-drove or clouted the turning ball beyond the boundary. Dubbed slog sweeps by the pundits, these clean, calculated blows were better than slogs, certainly more controlled, and more dominating than cross-batted swings to leg.

The quality of this attack was a reminder of Botham's clean-hitting days at Australia's expense in 1981. Contemporarily only Chris Cairns, and his efforts have been spasmodic, has matched Gilchrist's exciting batting ability. His subsequent failures, and Laxman's

English umpire David Shepherd reflects the cricketer's superstition about the number 111, and does a jig, going up and down on his toes, until the score changes. Superstitious teams have been known to keep their feet off the floor in the dressing room until danger passes. Colloquially, cricketers refer to 111 as "Nelson", a reference to Admiral Horatio Nelson's physical condition ... one eye, one arm, and one other part of the anatomy, which broadcasters translate to "one opinion". Historically Australians refer to 87 as a jinx number, although the statistics fail to bear this out.

exhilarating 281 in Calcutta, revealed the extremes of batting as cricket's primal force.

Gilchrist made a king pair in Calcutta, and one in each innings in Chennai, failing to deal with Harbhajan's arm ball. Arguably he had used up all his luck in one innings. More likely he proved again that the scale of vulnerability starts at 100 per cent from the first ball, reducing quickly to half that number within three or four overs, depending on the bowlers.

In Calcutta he was certainly unlucky in the first innings, because the ball pitched outside the leg stump. In the second innings, as Australia collapsed under the weight of a baying crowd and that calamitous in-between dilemma of attack or defence, he swept injudiciously and missed. His failures also reminded everyone how important his dynamic batting had been in the course of 16 consecutive victories.

Laxman's innings soared to the other extreme of batting primacy, reaffirming the delight of cricket's unpredictability, and the fickleness of human nature.

He arrived in the middle of Eden Gardens with India at one for 52 in its second innings, and still double "David Shepherd" – 222 runs that is – behind. Last man out for 59, and he probably wasn't, in India's awful first innings capitulation for 171 in 58 overs, Laxman was presciently promoted to number three.

His first scoring shot went past mid-off for four, and by the close of the third day he had reached a memorable hundred, with another 16 boundaries.

Australia's bowlers reckoned they were only one wicket away from another Indian slide, but not a chance went to hand during the epic marathon partnership between Laxman and Dravid on the fourth day, which was certainly a case of rising from the dead.

Perched in the alfresco ABC commentary box, which was at a Laxman deep long-on for half of the match, and a late-cut third man for the rest, the chanting, urging crowd banged our ears, and created the atmosphere that a broadcaster dreams about.

Like Sulla at the Colosseum, the electronic scoreboard announced tributes to the Indian gladiators as they, particularly Laxman, marched past landmarks.

Dining out with some Indian family friends, Subimal and Chitra Ghosh, that night, I was assured that this metamorphosis would be completed with an Indian victory. Politely, I demurred, suggesting India would bat too long, and in any case the pitch was too good to dismiss Australia in less than a day.

Folly. The game is played more in the head than elsewhere, and unused to a match-saving situation, Australia, as I had been told, collapsed.

This notion of batting's primacy had struck home on February 26th when my phone rang at two in the morning in Mumbai with the ABC news of Sir Donald Bradman's demise.

Bradman had transformed the game with his phenomenal batting. And he scored at such a rapid rate, demoralising bowlers and captains who struggled to come up with countering tactics. Only the infamous Bodyline strategy depowered his scoring ability.

Steve Waugh's powers of concentration may be superior to any contemporary batsman; but Bradman's twinkle-toed footwork, range of shots and a remorseless hunger for scoring runs, were unique, and those famous numbers 99.94, Bradman's Test average, are a statistical epitaph of his greatness

And the numbers live on as the address for the ABC – Box 9994 in your capital city. Given the ABC's lengthy commitment to cricket coverage from the earliest days of radio in Australia, and Bradman's contribution to our sense of nationhood, it seems an appropriate feature of our daily communication.

And while the teams paid their respects by wearing black armbands on the opening day of the series in Mumbai, there was a sentimental perception that Bradman's phenomenal deeds could be inspirational.

Not everyone in the ABC box felt sentimental. But I did, and at that moment our listeners were probably a mob of "sentimental blokes".

Perched in the alfresco ABC commentary box, which was at a Laxman deep long-on for half of the match, and a late-cut third man for the rest, the sound of Calcutta's chanting, urging crowd banged our ears, and created the atmosphere that a broadcaster dreams about.

Early Days

IF I'D BEEN ASKED AS A YOUNG MAN ABOUT
THE PROSPECT OF GETTING A JOB AS A CRICKET
COMMENTATOR WITH THE ABC, IT WOULD
HAVE BEEN REMOTE. BUT LOOKING BACK TO
CHILDHOOD, THE GAME HAS BEEN PART OF MY
LIFE FOR ALMOST AS LONG AS I CAN RECALL.

Cricket has been good to me. I've been involved for over 28 years as a commentator on ABC Radio, and cricket has played a role for a lot longer than that, right back to my distant schooldays.

Growing up in Sydney's Eastern Suburbs, we were only a short bus ride from the SCG, but I didn't have much interest in cricket till I was about 10.

What triggered it was perhaps my father taking me to the Cricket Ground. While he watched the game I used to run around in the Members area, spending most of my time picking up those old Blue Bow soft drink bottles. I think Tooths had the licence for all beverage output at the SCG in those days, and every bottle you got was worth threepence.

The author, three years old.

There I'd be, ferreting around the Members all day looking for the bottles that people had left behind, then I'd whip them back and get some money on them. Later they brought in a rule that you had to buy another bottle every time you brought one back.

Perhaps it was at that point, when the commercial proceedings started to drop off a little, that I took more interest in the cricket.

A family and school friend, Tim Cohen, developed a growing interest in the cricket at the same time. We used to sit next to each other during the summer holidays scoring at the Sheffield Shield matches.

A few of those old scorebooks are still somewhere around the house. Full Test matches and Sheffield Shield matches kept us occupied, and when there was no cricket on we were round at his place in the backyard playing our own Test matches.

We played a little bit at my place, but we broke too many windows in the backyard there so we had to go out in the street. We devised a game where instead of risking damage with a hard ball we used a tennis ball. To take the bounce out of it we used to drop the ball in a bucket of water, just shake it off a bit and come in to bowl. It would hit the bitumen and come off at the same height as a normal cricket ball.

We set imaginary fields. Where we used to live up in Bellevue Hill there was a rockery wall on one side of the road, so we could run up one side of the street towards the corner and bowl across the street into this wall. We scratched out some stumps on the wall.

And we'd umpire our own games. It was fairly successful, there weren't too many disputes, though there were quite a few O'Neills and Harveys caught in unusual positions by very athletic fieldsmen.

We played Test matches like that every holidays for ages, right through the school years into our mid-teens. There were a number of summers up at Tim's parents' holiday place at Mona Vale as well. Mona Vale is on Sydney's Northern Beaches, so when it got too hot we just went off for a swim. Right until the time we left school we were still playing.

A serious interest in playing only emerged when I went into boarding school at Cranbrook. I boarded for four years, though we only lived a mile from school, but being an only child my parents thought it was a good idea, so I was there the last two years of junior and the first two of senior. Then I went back to being a day boy because I got sick of the closed-in routine.

At boarding school, every day after school we'd be

Say so... "*Those were lovely, light-headed, easy-going days, where you could get away with having a lot of fun playing sport and not worrying too much about study. That was the thing you did the night before the exam.*"

on the oval. If we weren't in the team practice, and I wasn't in any teams of significance in those days, we would just invent our own games. We'd do that every afternoon, and on Saturdays and Sundays. There was a lot of opportunity to play games, that's probably what excited my interest. I went from the 13Fs and Es up to the 14As and 15As, so it really developed pretty quickly.

Those were lovely, light-headed, easy-going days, where you could get away with having a lot of fun playing sport and not worrying too much about study. That was something you did a couple of days or maybe the night before an exam. And that pretty much happened all the way through. There wasn't the pressure to pass exams.

What I really enjoyed was captaining teams. I started with the 15As, I think, then I went up to the Seconds, had one game, then I played in the Firsts in 1966 and '67, and I was captaining in my last year in '68, when I went back and repeated.

An all-rounder of sorts, I didn't have a lot of patience. My most memorable strokes have gone over fences, my least memorable ones have been clear quick ducks. I still remember in 1964 in the 14As hitting a ball into the Advanx Tyre Factory beside Sydney Grammar's Weigall ground in Rushcutters Bay. It went right across Neild Avenue, over the fence, into the factory. It was the only day I ever played at Weigall, which is curious because the ground is named after my great-grandfather, Albert Bythesea Weigall, the famous "Mr Chips" headmaster at Sydney Grammar.

As I said, captaining was what I enjoyed. I liked the tactical battles. And we were fortunate enough when I was at school to have some very good players. One in particular, Jerry Thiedeman, played in the NSW schoolboys team with Jeff Thomson. A left-arm spinner and a right-hand batsman, he was a high quality player.

From a captain's point of view, he was such a good bowler that on a turning pitch I often wouldn't have anyone on the on side. I'd have him make the batsman hit across the line, because he could turn the ball so much and bowl accurately. This was typical of the innovative tactics that appealed to me, with the help of senior players like Jerry and Tim Cohen.

We had four fast bowlers and Jerry and myself were the spin bowlers in the team. (One of the four quicks was Andrew Stathopoulos, who also represented Australia in the 1969 schoolboys rugby team. He achieved infamy later in life by embezzling Bishopsgate insurance for $27 million, and was last heard of incarcerated in a Greek jail.) So we had a pretty good run that last year, which was capped off by beating the Old Boys. This was always the big game of the year. It would go all day Friday, into Saturday, you'd break for

The name Weigall – my mother's family name – provides an unexpected link with cricket in addition to my great-grandfather's connection with the Weigall Ground in Sydney, where I played schoolboy cricket.

Gerry Weigall was a famous eccentric English cricketer in the early 1900s, and a relative of my mother's. She met him once on a trip to London. His story is detailed in "Great Characters from Cricket's Golden Age" by English writer Jeremy Malies. (Published in 2000 by Robson Books, London.) Weigall, who died in 1944 aged 73, was widely celebrated for his terse sayings, such as: "Never run on a misfield", "Never cut in May", "Never hook until you have made 84" and "Never play off the back foot from the bottom end at Canterbury". He was an accomplished player, but his cautionary remarks on running between the wickets were based on bitter experience. Playing for Cambridge University in the 1892 Varsity match, he was implicated in three run-outs. Said CB Fry, "This was the game in which the Cambridge player Gerry Weigall did more to win the match for Oxford than anyone on our side."

Going for Broke at 5 Cents a Pop

....

THE GAMES PEOPLE PLAY — WHEN THEY SHOULDN'T

As I admit elsewhere in this book, I make it a mission that I like to have a bet. Game playing, and the hazards of gambling, started early.

When I was at school I copied a cricket game from somewhere and refined it. The standard game was to take a six-sided pencil, mark the sides 1, 2, 3, 4, 6 and "out", and roll. Instant cricket, very simple.

While the French lesson was going on and you were bored out of your brain, you secured a good position at the back of the room, and using the incline on the desk, you just rolled the pencil.

The French droned on while you were writing the scores in your book.

My refinement of this was that instead of having "out" you'd have "appeal", and then a second pencil marked "lbw", "stumped", "run out", "bowled", "caught", or "not out". A friend alongside me would have the same thing going, so he'd play one innings and I'd do the other.

In a couple of French lessons you'd have a Test match. It was terrific, and far more interesting than French.

I've probably never stopped playing games to be honest. In my last years at school I used to run football cards, as well as bets on the racing. John Moore, the son of the famous jockey George Moore, was in my class and I used to try to get a bit of information out of him. But all that

> "THE SON OF JOCKEY GEORGE MOORE WAS IN MY CLASS AT SCHOOL. HIS DAD WAS AN APPALLING TIPSTER."

John knew came from his father and I learnt early on that jockeys deserve their renown as appalling tipsters. So it didn't help me much.

I got cleaned out in 1967 by a boy who was a keen student of the form. He got me on the Metropolitan, with a horse called Wiedersehen at 25-1.

I was taking five cent bets on races, and I think he had a whole 20 cents on at 25-1. Five dollars was a big payout in those days.

On the football cards there was a little bloke in second form who knocked me out one day: He got the whole card right, six matches, and it was 33-1 or something. I remember his name, and he probably remembers mine, he's still around the place somewhere. I don't know what he'd say about my early forays into bookmaking, I'm not sure I'd want him to.

He chased me round the school for a week before I could pay him out.

Say so... *"I went to the University of New South Wales after leaving school. The Randwick racecourse was over the road, life was pleasant, study was a huge distraction for the social activities. I failed every subject."*

Speech Day, and have two hours more play after that. This particular game is memorable because we'd lost on the first innings. We went out and had a hit on Saturday morning and had only an inconsequential lead really – I think we left them 120 to get after speech day.

There were one or two younger blokes, one in particular, in the side who criticised me for throwing the game away. I said, "Well, we've already lost on the first innings, what's it matter?"

As it turned out, we bowled them out in the fading light. But there was probably some complicity there with the umpires, who were World War I veterans. (See "Unforgettable Characters" overleaf).

I didn't play at uni, I played for the Old Cranbrookians Cricket Club. I went to the University of New South Wales and did first year Arts: Philosophy, History, an ersatz subject called the History and Philosophy of Science, which was a bridge between science and the humanities, and Political Science.

My mother was there at the same time studying Spanish. She's multilingual and had got sick of Italian – talking to the greengrocer wasn't quite wide enough a circle for her – and she discovered that Spanish had a bit more going for it in terms of the literature and the people involved. She has since made a lot of friends among migrants from South America in particular.

She probably had more interest in being at university than I did. The Randwick racecourse was over the road, life was pleasant, study was a huge distraction for the social activities. I failed every subject.

So the next year it was time to get a job. I started

with National Mutual Life working in their city office as a clerk in the superannuation department. If I'd been asked then, the prospect of my getting a job as a cricket commentator with the ABC would have been remote. But in some ways I was heading in that direction.

I listened to radio at home a lot. I was given an ancient Radiola at seven, tuning in to the serials and Gary O'Callaghan on 2UE Breakfast with Sammy the Sparrow. I can still remember in the early '60s sitting with my father listening to the crackling shortwave radio descriptions from England; I can remember Meckiff being no-balled out of Test cricket in '63-4, just sitting on a Saturday in the house listening to the radio, as today we might sit there watching television.

We hardly ever had television. We only used to get it at home as a treat for the holidays, because my parents

Unforgettable Characters

IF YOU THINK TODAY'S UMPIRES ARE A PROBLEM, YOU SHOULD HAVE BEEN AROUND IN MY SCHOOLDAYS. NO MATTER HOW ODD THEIR DECISIONS, YOU DIDN'T ARGUE.

Umpires and groundsmen, they were some of the great characters of my schooldays. We had all these octogenarian umpires. The two most famous were Mr Bockman and Mr Paris. Ernie Bockman had had a left testicle shot out at Ypres during World War I, and he tended to jump around the place a little bit.

His judgment was like his physical condition, a little unbalanced. He came up with some appalling decisions occasionally and we played on this.

And then there was Fred Paris, who'd had his arm shot off in the First World War, and he was known of course as the one-armed bandit. His biggest problem was signalling sixes. It was kind of a wave.

Between Mr Paris and Mr Bockman there were some very funny decisions given. Usually our way.

There was another chap, George, who was so old he'd sustain himself with a pack of biscuits, and he'd sit down at square leg between overs. He got me one day at Trinity, I still remember. I came in close to the stumps and I knocked the bails off as I bowled. He called "no ball" as the batsman was bowled over.

I said, "What was that for?"

He said, "You can't do that. You can't break the stumps."

didn't think it was a very good influence. They were very culturally minded, with a consuming interest in the classics and archeology; Dad was also one of the judges for the Playwrights' Advisory Board – he was one of the early advocates of "Summer of the Seventeenth Doll".

He had been an actor with Sydney University Dramatic Society years earlier and had acted with people like Dinah Shearing, Lynn and Betty Lucas, and Lyn Murphy, who became significant actors later on.

Later in his life Dad would talk about those early days of Australian acting. One of his school chums, Alan Davis, became a director in London, and produced the long-running West End hit "No Sex Please, We're British".

Dad obviously knew a lot of people who went on to make a career out of it, something I think he would have liked to have done. He went to England in '38,

"Well, you probably can't," I said, "but it's not a no ball."

He said, "I'm umpiring, get on with the game." That was that – you didn't argue with the umpires, did you? You were always taught that. Call it gratuitous grace.

The other great character in those formative days was George Eccles, who was four foot nothing and a magnificent groundsman. At Cranbrook we played on what was arguably one of the finest cricket pitches in Sydney – all the overseas players used to come to practise on it.

George used to roll it and roll it and roll it. It was too good really, you could almost see your face in it, he'd brought the mud up so much. They were beautiful strips to bat on, so true you could always be confident of hitting across the line towards New South Head Road.

George was a great favourite with the boys because he used to let them slip in the back of the little groundsman's shed and he'd play cockatoo if you wanted to have a smoke down the back there.

He'd be having his lunch hour and he'd be lookout in case a prefect or a master came around.

The oval was certainly his territory. There was no way anyone could go on that oval until three o'clock when you had practice or a match was on. George used to spend a lot of time making sure the kids didn't go on it.

And he was a great swearer. I think that was the other thing that appealed to the impressionable kids at school. He was the first bloke that put "f" and "c" together on a regular basis – he embellished almost every expression, except when he was talking to the headmaster.

He was a lovely man but he was very earthy ... extremely earthy ... the green-fingered George Eccles.

having got a law degree, but his father died suddenly and he had to come home and take over the law practice. Then the War came. But he always retained his interest in history, the arts and in acting.

He was a keen cricketer and a secretary of the I Zingari Cricket Club for a long while, and we used to play in the backyard quite a bit, but his brother was a much better cricketer than Dad. Uncle Ham had played grade cricket for Paddington.

As I've said, my interest in cricket had grown at school, and not just in playing.

One of the things I did was to bring out my own cricket magazine, "Cricket Chronicle". Mum used to type it up on the typewriter with carbon copies, six at a time, and I used to sell it for five cents.

It was about four or five pages with comment, and I used to give incentives like a quiz and crossword with a prize to the winner. That went on for a couple of years off and on, when the mood took me.

Around 1967, while I was still at school, a job came up in the ABC and I applied for it. I didn't even get an interview, but one of the fellows who had preceded me at Cranbrook, a very good sportsman called Peter Meares, got the job.

Then in 1969, when I was at uni, another one came up. Another application, and this time I think I even got to the interview stage. It was quite an intensive process of selection and there was a first round of quiz questions or general knowledge sports questions that I didn't manage to get past. And that was the job that gave Gordon Bray, who was later to become the voice of rugby union on Channel 7, his start in broadcasting.

Throughout this period I had an ambition to be a cricket commentator, knowing that the opportunities would only come up occasionally to join the only organisation that provided traineeships, the ABC.

By 1971 I was getting restless at National Mutual, and I went to work for Amev Life, a Dutch insurance

Say so... *"One of the things I did at school was to bring out my own cricket magazine. 'Cricket Chronicle'. Mum used to type it up on the typewriter with carbon copies, six at a time, and I used to sell it for five cents."*

company, again just in a clerical position. I'd been there six months or so, winding along, and I ran into Tom Spencer, a former workmate at National Mutual who played first grade with Manly.

"You're keen on your cricket," he said. "There's a big tour coming up to England."

The Australian Old Collegians had been organising amateur cricket tours overseas since the 1950s. I decided that this was too good an opportunity to miss, and I went off on that tour in 1972.

We went round the world playing cricket – Honolulu, the United States, Canada, Bermuda, England – it was wonderful. The team played 90 matches in five months.

We were based in London for a month, then we went to Geneva, Monte Carlo and Rome.

After Rome, the boys went on to Hong Kong and then home, but I stayed on and went back to London, where I shared a flat with a couple of cricketers who played for Queensland and were over there for a while: John Maclean and John Loxton.

It was the year of the Munich Olympics, and I stayed in England until that finished. By now money was getting low and it was time to head for home. I got a cheap fare on British Caledonian to Perth, where there was a girlfriend I wanted to catch up with.

On the way I stopped off in Singapore for one night, and there was a memorable guy on the bus, full of beans, singing and getting everyone to sing as we went from the airport to the hotel. He was quite impressive. It turned out later that his name was John Farnham – my brush with fame.

It cost a few hundred quid to get to Perth, and that was it, I'd run out of dough. There was nothing for it

From the Scrapbook

ONE OF THESE DAYS I'M GOING TO HAVE A CLEAROUT...

The author in action, 1969.

Safari-shirted in the Caribbean in the 1980s.

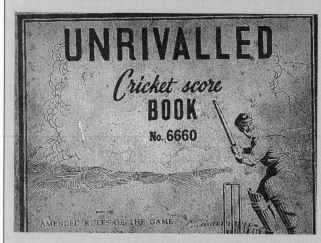

The trusty scorebook that accompanied me on visits to the SCG back in the 1960s.

Canbrook v Sydney Grammar in 1965.

The editor speaks out, 1967.

Say so... *"I'd been away for about six months, I was broke and with no real expectations. And the day I got home my mother said ... You know that job at the ABC, those traineeships? Well, another one has come up."*

but to ring my father and say I'm down to my last couple of cents, can you shout me a trip back home on the Indian Pacific? He came to the rescue.

I remember sitting on the train watching the spinifex and the monotonous desert landscape, as we went bouncing along the Nullarbor Plain for about two days. It was very dreary.

I just wanted to get home. I'd been away for about six months, I was broke and with no real expectations of what was going to happen next.

And on the first day home my mother said, "You know that job in the ABC, those traineeships you were keen on getting? Well, another one has come up."

The process of applying for the job took a while, and in the intervening period I went off to New Zealand with the Old Boys team on their first overseas tour. The trip was paid for on a lucky collect from a second placing in a Melbourne Cup sweep, the lightweight Alsop chasing Rain Lover to the post.

Peter Meares, who by then was something of a fixture in the ABC, was on the tour with us, and he gave me a few clues about how to broadcast cricket.

I thought I knew it all of course. He said, "You should think about doing it this way," adding, "This is what McGilvray said to me..." and so on.

We sat on the edge of the ground a couple of times and I just made up the commentary. His advice was very useful for the audition that came later.

From the original list of 100 applicants the field was reduced to three for the final audition. The ABC gave me a choice of going to White City to do tennis or an audition at a cricket match. I chose the cricket, a Test match between Australia and Pakistan at the SCG.

Two months later, April 1973, I started work as a trainee sports commentator with the ABC.

A New Season

THE WEST INDIES, INDIA, ENGLAND:
NEAR NON-STOP CRICKET BECKONED IN THE
COMING SUMMER AND BEYOND. THE GREATEST
QUESTION OF ALL WAS HOW FAR AUSTRALIA
COULD STRETCH ITS WINNING RUN.

Octanober 15, 2000. A serene Sunday at North Sydney for New South Wales's first one-day match against Victoria. It is the start of the 2000/01 season. Remove the trappings of one-day hoopla, and North Sydney Oval transports you to a gentler, friendlier era of cricket's timelessness. My eyes drift around the ground's Victorian-style architecture: the Macartney and O'Reilly stands with their intimate seating, close enough for theatrical amusement and interaction; the Bob Stand, transported from the Sydney Cricket Ground 20 years ago, its ancient housing cheerfully relocated. There it is today in the shade of North Sydney's most identifiable landmark, the huge Moreton Bay fig tree that defies big hitters to whack the ball over its crown.

As the players take the field – I'm in the box on commentary duty – I have a few minutes to think of the summer of cricket in store. Ahead there will be the five Test match home series against the West Indies, and afterwards, starting on January 12, the Carlton and United one-dayers, a three-sided contest including Zimbabwe. Beyond that lies our tour of India, and mid-2001 we're off to England.

Like every Australian cricket fan, I relish the prospect of seeing Steve Waugh's champions doing battle with the likes of Brian Lara, Courtney Walsh and Sachin Tendulkar, not to mention the small matter of England and the Ashes.

Equally, like everyone who's been in Sydney over the past month, I have become a gourmet of sporting excellence. It's only a couple of weeks ago that the world's Olympians packed their bags and headed for home – any one of 200 nations – leaving behind a sizeable swag of gold, silver and bronze dangling around Aussie necks.

That sports carnival in Sydney was preoccupying most of us when Australia's cricketers slipped away late in September to Kenya. They were to play in a one-day

Dr Grace and those colonials

······················

"WG" MADE TWO CONTROVERSIAL AUSTRALIAN TOURS.

I've made many English friends through the years thanks to cricket, but there's a certain sort of Pom that still gets under the skin. The name Geoff Boycott comes to mind among others — as bloody-minded as they come in my opinion.

Nothing new in that. More than 100 years ago the famous Dr WG Grace was admired as a cricketer, but was judged overbearing and petty by many Australians.

He visited twice: in 1873-4 and 1891-2. Perhaps understandably he took exception to the Australian practice of moving from a rough to smooth pitch for the home team's innings. And there was much talk of the Australians failing to abide by the umpires' decisions.

In 1873 the Melbourne Cricket Club invited Grace to raise a side. He was offered second-class passage and the paltry fee of 170 pounds. He was allowed very generous expenses, provided he played in every match. Grace was also on his honeymoon, though Agnes Grace stayed mainly with friends in the large cities, while her husband was tirelessly scoring 758 runs at 39, and taking 65 wickets at 7.4. The team won 12 of their 15 matches, against odds of 18 and 22 opponents, and found time to hunt rabbits, pigeons, kangaroo, quail, plover and goldfish.

Travelling by Cobb coach on rough bush tracks must have been exhausting, coping with the extremes of heat, dust, flies and then drenching rain. And some of the pitches were crook. Grace reported that a bushel of pebbles (several buckets) was collected from a pitch in Tasmania before they could play.

The rancorous nature of the tour meant that Grace didn't return to Australia until Lord Sheffield persuaded him to, aged 43, in 1891-2. He was paid three thousand pounds, plus expenses, plus a locum for his practice in Gloucestershire.

The arrival of the railway system made for more comfortable travel around a country that had become highly urbanised and industrialised, adopting the telegraph and the telephone soon after Britain.

In 27 matches Grace's team lost only twice; beaten in the first two of three Tests. Grace headed the batting averages in the eight first-class games, scoring 448 runs at 44.80. Despite high attendances the tour was a financial flop for the sponsor, Lord Sheffield, who lost two thousand pounds.

Sheffield's legacy was the creation of a perpetual trophy for intercolonial matches; a trophy that was competed for until 1999-2000.

The apocryphal story of Grace replacing the bails after being bowled and, refusing to leave, declaring, "They've (the crowd) come to see me bat, not you bowl," shows how he saw himself as the highest paid amateur sportsman of the era.

Say so... ... on being named in the "Team of the 20th Century"...

" I think this country is the greatest cricketing country in the world. We have proved we are the best there has ever been." **Neil Harvey**

cricket tournament in Nairobi, the ICC KnockOut 2000, ostentatiously billed as the Mini World Cup. Taking part along with Australia were India, New Zealand, South Africa, Pakistan, England, Zimbabwe, Sri Lanka, Bangladesh and West Indies.

The Aussies' one-day record was a good one: at home the world champions had lost only one of their 10 matches against Pakistan and India the previous summer, overwhelming India four times.

In New Zealand, back in March, they won the one-day contests 4-1. But since then they had played only an off-season tournament against South Africa, in which they lost three of the six matches.

Nothing could be taken for granted in Nairobi. Australia was drawn against India in its first match, the quarter final. Two years ago, in 1998, in their corresponding first-round match at the exotically named Bangabandhu Stadium in Dhaka, Bangladesh, I had seen Australia's bowlers being Tendulkarised, and the team eliminated.

The plan in Nairobi was to put in some gruelling practice sessions, then wind down and relax. It sounded good, imitating the methods of successful teams in other sports, who can switch the on/off buttons accordingly. However, like the golfer who tunes his game on the practice range knowing the time is only well spent if your score improves, the switching method is only justified by performance.

The Aussies warmed up with a couple of matches against the locals ... maybe a bit like those ancient games between Dr Grace and the twenty-two of Ballarat in the 1880s (see opposite for more about the visit of the good doctor) ... maybe Kenya's status would grow as rapidly as Australia's had in the days before

The star of India's quarter final victory over Australia was Yuvraj Singh, an 18-year-old from India's under-19 World Cup winning team, and a batsman with the reach of Graeme Pollock and the wristy fluency of an Azharuddin. His 84 off 80 balls was preceded by Tendulkar's 38 from 37, including some smashes off McGrath. The Narromine express went for a wicketless 61 from nine overs, including an edged boundary from Singh's singeing bat that Mark Waugh at slip didn't lay a hand on. Maybe his back was hurting.

Waugh's aches, Harvey's tender shoulder, Warne's absence for a knee operation ... incipient signs for some selection refreshment? Worst of all Australia didn't bowl their overs in time, and were docked two in the chase.

A week or so later India reached the final against New Zealand, having defeated South Africa in the semi-final. The final on October 15 resulted in a win for New Zealand. India batted first and scored 264, setting the Kiwis a target of only one run less than they'd set Australia a week earlier. Chris Cairns's commanding 102 runs from 113 was enough to make the difference, securing the KnockOut Cup, with two balls and four wickets to spare.

Federation when the cartoons depicted a kangaroo tugging at a lion's tail.

The 2000 version of a cricketing kangaroo went on a wild dog tour of Kenya's Masai mara, where catching wild dogs or lions proved to be just as difficult as dismissing the legendary doctor in his heyday. In fact most of the catching was done on mini video cameras, the tourist toys that have long since replaced the shotgun on shooting safaris. The lion ate the wildebeest, the cameras captured the Masai children at play, and according to plan the players relaxed before returning to face India.

Back at Nairobi, distractingly, the revelations about match-fixing were thick around the Indian team, who were keen to move on under Ganguly's leadership without the baggage of the disgraced Azharuddin and Jadeja in the dressing room.

For the Australians, memories of the first-round defeat two years earlier were all the more incentive for a revenge victory in Nairobi. And a step towards winning another trophy, which would confirm the team's champion status.

They batted second and lost by 20 runs, chasing an Indian total of 265.

It was a poor result given the pace of the chase during a Ponting/Bevan partnership of 73. The innings fell away when Robin Singh took a blinder to dismiss Ponting for 46, and Bevan was run out for 42 by India's new batting star, Yuvraj Singh. India were brilliant in the field, taking every chance.

Steve Waugh's summary was typically to the point – accurate and honest as always.

"That was a perfect batting wicket for a small

Say so... *"No, I don't look at myself as an understudy ... Perhaps I will be eternally short of opportunities due to the fact that Warney is the preferred wrist-spinner in Australia."* **Stuart MacGill**

In a spin

TWO GIFTED SPINNERS ... ONE PLACE IN THE TEAM

The author interviews Warne

Shane Warne's future, and the simmering rivalry between him and fellow leggie Stuart MacGill, took centre stage two weeks into the season. Warne sustained a break to his finger in the Pura Cup match between Victoria and NSW at Punt Road Oval, when attempting to take a miscued skied shot from Mark Waugh. He took the catch but in the process fractured and dislocated the top knuckle of the third finger, an injury that would put him out of action for six to eight weeks.

All of a sudden Stuart MacGill, the man in waiting, was going to get a saloon passage into the Test team. With Warne's injury he was in a position where he could really stake a claim, and certainly on his record from 12 Test matches of 59 wickets at an average of just over 23, he had already proved himself as a quality wrist-spin bowler.

He did realise that in order to prove himself he'd have to take wickets consistently, and then the crunch might come.

If so, which one of the two bowlers would it be?

"I don't look at myself as an understudy," MacGill said in a newspaper interview. "I look at it this way. Perhaps I will be eternally short of opportunities due to the fact that Warney is the preferred wrist-spinner, but as long as I stay fit and patient, the opportunities will come."

MacGill clearly felt that with a powerful performance he might in the longer term have been seriously able to rival Warne. But I think the feeling among most of the players, and certainly the commentators, was that as soon as Warne was fit he'd walk straight back into the team. The question mark lingered as it had at other stages in Warne's career when he'd suffered injuries, a shoulder injury in particular, that appeared to detract from his ability to take wickets, and the sceptics were saying again — well, will he come back from this injury?

They were underestimating the powers of a champion. As the months rolled on, and despite MacGill's creditable performance in four Test matches with 16 wickets at 31.31, it became quite clear that Warne was determined to regain his rightful position as the No 1 spin bowler in the side, and he made a tremendous physical commitment to keeping himself in the shape.

MacGill's patience would be tested yet again.

What was the lesson to be learnt by Australia from the disappointment? More hunger. Indulge in the luxuries after the victory, not before. Bring on the shrinks.

ground. Three hundred was a pass score ... our batting wasn't good enough."

Waugh has always been practical, pragmatic. So what was the lesson to be learnt from this disappointment?

More hunger. Indulge in the luxuries of local culture *after* the victory. Setting high standards imposes a discipline that can be more easily disturbed in one day than five. Whereas a bad session in a Test can be influential, in a 50-over game it's normally fatal.

Bring on the shrinks.

In all its unpredictability, cricket is an expression of individualism subservient to a sense of team and corporate glory. The focus went missing in the Kenyan savannah. Back to basics. Back, in a manner of speaking, to Bankstown.

Back to the Blues, and that early summer's day at North Sydney. The Victorians, or Bushrangers according to cricket's latter-day marketing spruikers, had been coming north since intercolonial rivalries between the country's major cities began in 1856. If you carry a name like Bushrangers, you're asking for trouble.

In a throwback to the Kelly days at Glenrowan the men in blue ambushed the bushwackers, with Mark Higgs's deadly accurate throws disposing of two victims, run out, in a Victorian innings that did well to reach 193.

Brad Hodge crisply worked the bowling around the shorter boundaries for 87, reminding us of the talent that had spectacularly launched his career as a youth.

MacGill dipped his leg breaks expertly, and turned them lusciously. A full toss undid rival Shane Warne, who obligingly hit it straight back.

When the champion leggie bowled he looked seriously underdone, making his return from knee surgery earlier in the year.

He didn't have many runs to defend, and NSW batsman Brad Haddin's assault was furious,

Say so... *after Australia's loss by 20 runs to India at Nairobi...*

"*That was a perfect batting wicket for a small ground. Three hundred was a pass score ... our batting wasn't good enough.*" **Steve Waugh**

out-slathering his partner Slater in a run-a-ball chase that overhauled the target for a comfortable bonus point for the home side.

One of the recent changes to the laws of cricket was quadruply evident on the small North Sydney arena.

In the interests of uniformity, the rewritten laws of the game stipulate that the boundary was now defined by a line, not a fence, as had become the custom in over 100 years of the Australian game.

So any hit that crashed into the fence on the full was worth six. The gutter was the new defining line, which also meant fielders could no longer lean on the fence to claim a catch.

And they might be less inclined to slide into the fence to prevent boundaries, as Ricky Ponting had done so disastrously at the SCG in the one-day finals in January 2000, busting his ankle.

The radio descriptions "he's rattled the pickets" or "that one's cleared the fence" now seemed redundant, vanquished from the lexicon like zac and dina had disappeared in 1966 with the advent of decimal currency.

In the larger scheme of things, the MCC lawmakers' concern with fencing was trivial compared to the problems that confronted the ICC, who were doing their utmost to have conspiracies and corruption proscribed.

The ICC had held meetings in Nairobi, where the head of the Anti-corruption Unit, Sir Paul (later Lord) Condon, envisaged a long fight against the corrupting influences in the game.

At least the fight was going to be fought. The ICC's lack of vigilance and inertia had allowed the problem of match-fixing and corruption to fester, and at last a will and a process was apparent. But as we watched events, I certainly wasn't alone in thinking there was still a long way to go.

Take the confidential declarations that we were told would be required from players and officials, for instance – little more than another belated curiosity.

The proposed questionnaire sought information from any player, official or employee of the game, about instances of match-fixing, bribery or other breaches of the Code of Conduct. Heavy penalties were threatened for "incorrect" responses.

Would potential felons fess up?

Steve Waugh summed up, accurately, again.

"It's a good idea but I don't think it's going to make any difference ... if you've got nothing to hide you're not going to write anything down, and if you've got something to hide what's going to make you write that down and say you've been guilty if you haven't owned up to it already?"

Call an amnesty? Call the cops.

Well intended, the questionnaires were unlikely to provide as much ammunition for Condon as the series of investigations conducted by his incorruptible team,

Web of corruption

HAVE WE REALLY GOT TO THE BOTTOM OF THE SCANDALS? OR ARE THERE SOME VERY LUCKY CRICKETERS AROUND?

People ask me what I know about the extent of gambling and corruption in world cricket. My answer, like most people who've been close to the game, is not as much as I thought.

I know one Indian bookmaker who has been to Australia and has confirmed that there are unbelievable amounts of money going around. Everyone has completely underestimated how much is involved.

As an example, I was told that when Sanath Jayasuriya, the Sri Lankan captain, was in Sharjah in the last year or two he was invited to meet somebody for a special, but unspecified reason. I think he knew full well what was coming.

The first offer for the "development of a relationship" was $US250,000.

Say so... ... *on the proposed player's "declarations" about bribery ...*
*"If you've got something to hide, what's going to make you say you've been
guilty if you haven't owned up to it already?"* **Steve Waugh**

and the busy contingent of Cronje cops in India.

Of the Australian players touched by the scandals, Mark Waugh feels particularly hard done by. His reputation has been tainted because of a relationship he had with a bookmaker, as has Shane Warne's.

I tend to believe it was all fairly innocent but whether or not it continued beyond the point at which Mark said it ended was an interesting point that was only resolved after the ICC's inquiries brought down their findings in his favour.

At the end of the day, given the various terms of reference, the buck is going to end with the various national cricket boards. It will be up to them to do what's needed.

And I have the feeling unless it's a case like Hansie Cronje, cricket's watchdogs will prefer to let it pass. They'll hope that most of the players who have been involved in this sort of business are out of the game

Jayasuriya said he didn't want to have anything to do with this man, or anything that could bring the game into disrepute or tarnish his own reputation.

The man said, "All right, $US500,000." Jayasuriya said no again.

At which point the man said, "If you ring Mr Azharrudin, I think you'll find he'll vouch for me ... "

Those kinds of numbers alone give some idea of what's around. Someone has to be making an awful lot of money out of it. And the frightening part of it all is that you really don't know where it starts or finishes. There's still a feeling around that you can't believe what anyone says.

This is particularly true in Sharjah, the Gulf state that has been one of the real problem areas for the game. There may be genuine cricket lovers there, but it appears that others are more taken with the betting than the playing side of it. Now India has decided it will not play Pakistan there, in fact the Indian government has decreed that because of political tensions they're not going to play against them anywhere.

Say so... *"I wonder whether the West Indies have this rapport, or the Poms, or New Zealand. Do they have this rapport as Australian cricket has with its history?"* **Allan Border**

The uneasy political relationship between India and Pakistan brought problems to international cricket, most recently underlined by the terrorism crisis. Since India won the World Cup in 1983 their administrators invested heavily in the one-day game, and their Test match cricket suffered as a result. The ICC Chairman, Australian Malcolm Gray, expressing his personal views at the end of the tournament in Nairobi, pointed to the proliferation of one-day matches that were purely driven by money. The electronic media, the needs of pay television audiences, the massive market, the sponsors queuing up, all of this had increased the risk of corruption. To address the problem it became clear that something was crystallising within the ICC in terms of a rolling Test championship. There would be a roster that would ensure that everyone played everyone else on a regular basis, hopefully creating a better balance in Test match competition, and a reduction in the number of one-day matches. But here the India v Pakistan problem crops up again. If two nations are barely on speaking terms, how can cricket hope to have them play each other? And if two key teams aren't in the comp, how can it work as a world championship?

now. Let's hope they put in place a penal code that will prevent anyone from being tempted.

Until then the feeling will linger that not all has been allowed to be made public. I believe there has been a cover-up, and I think there are quite a few South African players, for instance, who have escaped penalty. From what I've heard, a number of their players have been very heavily involved and they got off. It's a few people rather than the whole team, and it's easy to moralise about these things – human foibles, greed, easy money – but there's still a lot of baggage and someone needs to sort it out.

In the end, who actually knows? The players who are involved within each team would know, but outside they'd only know as much as someone else has told them. As for me, I don't know what to believe any more and I think that goes for many of us.

I'd seriously like to believe that every time Australia go out to play the game's fair dinkum. I can't think of anything in recent times that would make me think otherwise.

And the game is amazingly resilient. Look at the two unforgettable Test matches that took place in India later in the season. Was there ever a hint that those games at Calcutta and Chennai had been fixed in some way? That India only came back into the contest because Australia had decided to take a million dollars from a bookmaker? I don't think so.

Thrown cricket matches weren't the ICC's only dilemma. Bowlers throwin' had been a problem since they were allowed to sling 'em down from above the

waist in the 1850s. Attempts to define a legal delivery
... "the ball shall be bowled, not thrown or jerked ... a
straightening of the elbow immediately prior to the
instant of delivery shall constitute a throw" ... had
more often confused the interpretation of what was a
fair delivery, making the umpires less inclined to make
a judgment on what was patently a chuck.

And as the paid, subservient implementers of the
legislation, the umps were more likely to turn a blind
eye, or maybe write a report, than stick out the arm of
denouement. Except for one. Darrell Hair.

He'd become public umpire/enemy number one in
Sri Lanka when he no-balled the contortionally wristed
off-spinning freak Muthiah Muralidaran at the MCG
in a Test match in 1995, and more recently he'd called
the occasional Zimbabwean left-arm tweaker Grant
Flower in a Test against New Zealand.

From "Fix" to Farce

The thing with cricket and gambling
is that it's so easy to fix any given
moment in the game. Think of all
the simple things that would be
completely undetectable.
Even before the game starts – who's
going to win the toss? Who's going to
be in the team?
In the first over, for instance, will the
bowler start with a wide ball?
You can't get those sorts of bets in
Australia, but you can in the
subcontinent. And unfortunately the
perception a lot of people seem to
have about the game is that it's a fix.
I've never thought this when watching
Australia play. I think the most farcical
thing I heard was Salim Malik alleging
that in a game in Sri Lanka some years
ago in a triangular series involving Sri

Lanka, Pakistan and Australia, it
wasn't only Pakistan who were trying
to throw the game but also Australia.
Just the picture the commentary ...
"Glenn McGrath has got the ball, he
runs in and bowls ... he's bowled a
wide, it's miles outside the off stump
... and Salim Malik has hit it straight
up in the air, it has gone over
backward point ... and Ricky Pointing
is down at third man ... he's under it,
it's a sitter, an absolute sitter ... oh,
he's dropped it, and not only dropped
it, he's picked it up ... and, this is
incredible, he's thrown it over the
fence ... six overthrows ...
"What will the umpire do about this?
Wait ... umpire Javed Akhtar, the well-
known Pakistani umpire, he's ... he's
signalling dead ball!"

Darrell had always stood his ground, defending the umpire's right to call the game as he sees it. And in Nairobi, as the knockout was warming up, he'd been rostered for the match between Sri Lanka and Pakistan. A diplomatic blunder by the ICC? Perhaps.

Fearing that Darrell might call their star bowler again, the Sri Lankans objected, and citing an administrative "misprint" in the programme, the ICC made a swap. The Hair "appointment criteria" were later explained by ICC chief executive David Richards, who said that the ICC had a policy of avoiding areas of potential conflict.

Sounded to me like Neville Chamberlain revisited. The Sri Lankans must have felt relieved, and omnipotent. And proving that one umpire's call was just a flirtatious matter of opinion, Grant Flower was

Darrell undaunted

AUSSIE UMPIRE DARRELL HAIR WILL GO DOWN IN HISTORY AS THE MAN WHO NO-BALLED SRI LANKAN SPINNER MURALIDERAN FOR CHUCKING AT THE MCG IN 1995.

Umpire Darrell Hair won't forget the 1995 Boxing Day Test match at the MCG when he called Muralidaran for throwing – on the first day there were over 50,000 fans there.

The pressure on umpires in such a situation is intense. In an environment where historically they have felt a lack of support from the administrators and have survived, or had at that time, on the captains' reports, it might be understandable on occasions to keep your head down, or your arm down, if you wanted a future.

Thoughts of self-preservation would only be human for fear of copping some retribution from the Sri Lankan players, the captain or the Sri Lankan captain's match report.

If Darrell Hair entertained such thoughts, history only records the simple fact of what happened. Out went the arm.

I talked to him after the event and there was no doubting the intensity of the feelings that had been aroused. Among the issues was a degree of disappointment felt by Darrell because his fellow umpire, New Zealander Steve Dunne, who had stood with him in Sharjah in previous months, had also expressed his doubts about the legality of Muralidaran's action. Yet when, after Darrell called Murali, the Sri allowed to bowl in his next match, without any apparent modifications to his action.

At the conclusion of the Nairobi event the ICC decreed that their advisory panel would assume power over bowlers who had been reported or called, overriding the authority of the home boards. An optimistic sign of ICC leadership. The world watches.

If throwing and match fixing stay on top of the agenda at future ICC executive meetings, they should let Darrell deal with the corrupters, and Sir Paul straighten the crooked elbows.

Lankan captain Arjuna Ranatunga decided he'd try his bowler out at the other end, Steve Dunne didn't call him. Perhaps he felt he was not in a position to assess the legality of Murali's action, perhaps he had changed his mind on the matter.

To put the throwing issue another way, the Australian coach, Bob Simpson, was quite adamant about Muralidaran in my discussions with him. He felt that he was a blatant chucker, and that he shouldn't be allowed to continue to play. Or at least there should be some process put in place in order to have his action remodelled.

So much at the time had been said about the fact that he had a deformity in his wrist and elbow that caused him to deliver the ball in such a peculiar fashion – but deformity or not, it still looked like an illegal delivery.

The problem with this is that since 1996 he has been able to continue with the Sri Lankan team and as far as Sri Lanka is concerned it's been just as well that he was part of their attack, because without him they wouldn't have been as competitive as they've been in a lot of Test matches. He has added great value to their cricket and to the game —if you can ignore the fact that it still looks as though most of his deliveries are illegal. This is of course a matter of opinion – and some politics.

It would seem that Muralidaran is clear now to play on, without being likely to cop the censure of an umpire or a match referee's report. It has gone past the point of no return. He has over 350 Test wickets and at his current rate could end up with 700 or 800 of them.

Were there consequences for Darrell Hair? Interestingly, and perhaps coincidentally, he was not selected for appointment in the World Cup in the subcontinent some months later.

West Indies

AN ENTIRE GENERATION OF AUSTRALIAN TEST
CRICKETERS WERE BLOODED, SOMETIMES
LITERALLY, BY THE GREAT WEST INDIES TEAMS
OF THE 1980S AND EARLY '90S. THESE VISITORS
WERE A SOMEWHAT DIFFERENT PROPOSITION.

The West Indies came to Australia with some very unconvincing international form and they started poorly in the series. However, the lead-up to the First Test match in Brisbane at the end of November was interesting.

A number of the surviving members of the West Indies and Australia sides from 1960-61 who had played in the tied Test match came to Brisbane for a nostalgic reunion. It was highlighted by a magnificent television programme, "Calypso Summer", created for the ABC by journalist Mike Coward and Lincoln Tyner, the ABC's special projects producer from Adelaide. They'd garnered interviews from most of the players who'd appeared in that famous game and linked those interviews with historic ABC footage of the match.

On the eve of the Test match, I attended a big dinner in Brisbane at which the 1960-61 players and the current players were the guests of honour.

Wes Hall, the great West Indies fast bowler of 40 years ago, was as ever the main and most amusing voice. He reminisced about an incident in the final over of the tied Test. Australia's Wally Grout had skied a ball and in the heat of the moment Wes charged out to square leg, where Rohan Kanhai was perched underneath it, ready to take a sitter. Hall came over the top of him and spilt the chance.

In a contritional moment he decided that after all these years he probably should apologise for what he had done. He even admitted to some sense of shame.

"I've been waiting 40 years for you to apologise for that, " Kanhai said, then through clenched teeth, "I'm grateful."

It was a well woven evening, with each ball of the final over being discussed by those who were involved. We were shown the footage from the programme, and then we'd come back for comments to those who played a part in each delivery. At the end of it, Mike Coward, the MC for the evening, replayed the whole of the final over one last time.

Richie Benaud, the Australian captain at that time, put it all in perspective. It's wonderful to be nostalgic,

The 2000-01 tour of Australia by the West Indies was the 20th Test series to be played since their first encounter in 1930-31.
The glory days of the 1980s and early '90s, when the West Indies had defeated Australia in five consecutive series, were long gone, indeed the team from the Caribbean had only a month or two earlier lost its most recent series 3-1 against England.
The overall statistics for Australia v West Indies at the start of the tour were:
Tests: 90;
Wins: Australia 37, West Indies 31;
Draws: 21;
Ties: 1.
Of the 52 Tests played in Australia, Australia had won 25, West Indies 18, with eight draws and one tie.

he said, but this should have no bearing on what's about to occur. We should all be mindful of the fact that this is a game that continues, and what's coming up is really what is the most important event. There's a Test match to be played.

I don't know how that went down with today's West Indies players, but as far as Australia was concerned Steve Waugh had certainly imbued his own players with a sense of the history and traditions of the game – most obviously in the past half-dozen years by establishing the Australian tradition of wearing their baggy green caps in the first fielding session of a match.

For the West Indies going into this Test match the signs weren't good. Brian Lara had played a couple of glittering innings in the lead-up in Western Australia and Alice Springs, but apart from that, one wondered how they were going to perform. We soon knew.

On the first day in Brisbane, Steve Waugh won the toss and put the opposition in. Knowing that the West Indies

Say so... *"Our bowlers showed they're capable of being very competitive and applying pressure to Australia. If we can get the score on the board we can apply more pressure."* **Coach Roger Harper**

batting was going to be under pressure in any circumstances, he backed a hunch and gave them first use of a pitch that might have had something in it. They succumbed meekly for 82.

It was an awful performance. In one-day parlance, they didn't even get their 50 overs, but were out in 49.1 overs in three-and-a-half hours of wretched batting. It was the lowest Test score at the 'Gabba for 50 years. McGrath, who bowled well but not brilliantly, had the remarkable figures of 20 overs, 12 maidens, 6-17. He was twice on a hat-trick.

Stuart MacGill, playing in place of the injured

Shane Warne, was the one who made the first break after the West Indies had batted for the best part of an hour. Campbell was caught by Mark Waugh at slip and that cued the collapse to McGrath. Brian Lara went for a duck.

The Australians responded strongly, with an excellent partnership between Hayden and Slater, who opened for only the second time in a Test match since being brought together in the Third Test at Hamilton, New Zealand, the previous season. They looked impressive, until there was a misunderstanding, perhaps a breakdown in communication between the two players who hadn't batted together a lot, and Hayden was run out for 44 when he looked well set.

At stumps on that first day Australia were in a wonderful position, with the night watchman Andy Bichel sent out to join Slater. Next day, Marlon Black bowled what was one of the better spells by a West Indies pace bowler in the whole series, pulling Australia back to 4-117. However, in the middle and lower order they got away again, thanks to Gilchrist's 48 and Brett Lee's unbeaten 62 from 80 deliveries.

Australia finished with 332, a significant lead that delivered them a comfortable victory on the third day. The match was all over 47 minutes before tea, Australia

Vintage Season

Exactly 40 years earlier, in 1960-61, the historic tour by the West Indies of Australia led to the establishment of the Frank Worrell Trophy in honour of the touring captain. Fondly remembered as the Calypso Summer, it was a vintage season, and an epic series between two great teams, including the nail-biting tied Test in Brisbane. Australia won the series 2-1. Australian players under captain Richie Benaud included Alan Davidson, Neil Harvey, Wally Grout, Norm O'Neill and Bob Simpson; West Indies captain Frank Worrell headed talents such as Garfield Sobers, Conrad Hunte, Wes Hall, Alf Valentine, Lance Gibbs, Gerry Alexander and Rohan Kanhai. In February 1961, at the end of the series, 500,000 people lined the streets of Melbourne to farewell Worrell and his team.

Keep talking!

....

RADIO IS INVISIBLE. SOMETIMES IT'S JUST AS WELL

When cricketing cronies get together, it's usually a time for reliving the highlights, and sometimes the low-lights. Old stories get trotted out, including the embarrassing ones. I was reminded of something that happened to me some years ago. A few listeners to ABC Radio may remember it too.

People come and go all the time in the box while we're broadcasting, some with unexpected consequences, such as members of the Maxwell family.

When my first son, Hamish, was two, I was baby-sitting while broadcasting at the Sydney Cricket Ground one Saturday morning. Mike Whitney, an expert commentator for us at the time, was supposed to be with me in the box, but he was delayed and for a while I was doing the broadcast on my own. I had to describe the game, watch the board and keep the broadcast moving along … at the same time keeping an eye on Hamish playing around the place.

I'd been on air for about 10 or 15 minutes when I felt Hamish moving closer towards me and I sensed that something was amiss.

He got closer and closer, and I thought, if I'm not careful he'll come in and say something on air, probably something I'll regret. My solution, and not a very effective one, was to keep going. I didn't realise at the time what his predicament was. Finally, he was only four or five inches away. I couldn't talk non-stop, sooner or later I had to draw breath. In that moment, I looked at Hamish, his eyes latched on to mine, and he seized his chance.

> I'D BEEN ON AIR FOR ABOUT 10 OR 15 MINUTES WHEN I SENSED THAT SOMETHING WAS AMISS. MY TWO-YEAR-OLD GOT CLOSER AND CLOSER...

"Daddy," he said, "I've got to do ukkies!"

I can't remember what I said — something like, "Oh excuse me, listeners" — but I spun round to the press box next door and said, "Help!"

Greg Growden, the sports journalist at *The Sydney Morning Herald*, came to the rescue while I staggered on with the commentary.

Whether Hamish has got a great sense of the dramatic or there was a physical need to do what he was talking about I don't know, but the upshot of it all was that while I kept the show on the road, he went off with Greg to the toilet and nothing happened. I think he was just taking the mickey out of dear old Dad.

Say so... *in an interview discussing the conditions in the West...*

"We have four fast bowlers dying to bowl in Perth. The toss really is luck and chance. The rest of the game isn't." **Coach Roger Harper**

winning by an innings and 126, with the West Indies once more capitulating, to McGrath (4 wickets) and Lee (3). Chanderpaul was the only one who offered any resistance, undefeated on 62, but he sustained an injury, one more in an injury-prone career. Sadly, it was to be the last time we'd see him in the series.

There were wonderful crowds in Brisbane – some 50,000 over the three days – with many people anticipating a strong West Indies showing. Instead they had recorded their 14th loss in 16 Tests away from home, while for Australia the victory delivered a record-equalling 11 Test wins in a row. Only one other team had ever achieved 11 straight wins in Test match cricket, ironically the West Indies.

By comparison, the current team was 6-81 at lunch on the third day, and the match didn't last long after that. One wag turned to me at lunch and said, "Can they lose another wicket during the lunch break?"

Two impressions stand out in my mind from the Second Test in Perth, one on-field, the other off.

After play on the second day we were given a rare insight into the relationship between Steve Waugh and his twin brother. That day Mark Waugh had scored a century, his 18th in Tests, composed and elegant as ever.

The most telling thing about his innings was that it had been made in the face of continuing allegations throughout the season of his involvement with an Indian bookmaker. Had he taken more money than he'd revealed?

The process of investigation from the ICC was taking its course, but opinion in the newspapers was

There was much talk during the early Test matches about the development of a new technology that was designed to help the umpires with lbw decisions. The innovation, to be called Hawkeye, was being considered by Channel Four in England. The plan was to have three cameras above the play, mounted so that they'd to be able to predict where the ball would have headed had the batsman's leg not impeded it. This would be three-dimensional, a step beyond the two-dimensional version already used on Channel Nine. Given the increasing reliance on the third umpire for run-outs and catches, one wondered whether the umpires would soon be much more than hatstands or ball counters. It seemed as though the drive to use technology was usurping all their power. I think even a number of players thought that this was an undesirable trend in the game, and one to be resisted.

divided. *The Australian* in particular was very, very hard on Mark, insisting that he should be stood down. The Fairfax newspapers, including *The Age* and *The Sydney Morning Herald*, believed the enquiry should be allowed to proceed and that everyone should wait for an outcome rather than jumping in at this stage. A fair bit of heat had built up.

And so it was a significant moment when the brothers stood together for the photographers and Steve said in that laconic way of his, "So what are we going to talk about?"

The body language was unmistakable; it was all about sympathy and care for the brother who he knew had been under an incredible amount of pressure. He felt a great deal of emotion towards Mark, and the importance of the century certainly wasn't lost on him.

Mark, he said, had a lot more mental toughness than he'd been given credit for over the years. In Steve's view, when their careers ended, people would recognise they were equally talented and equally mentally tough, though they might play in completely different ways.

On the field, the Second Test was memorable for a hat-trick by Glenn McGrath, the bowler who Dennis Lillee had recently said was quite capable of going to 500 wickets in his Test career.

Australia had won the toss, and with some bounce likely, Waugh had put the West Indies in.

By the ninth over of the match the visitors were 1-19. With McGrath bowling, Campbell steered one straight to Ponting at first slip. Next ball, with the slips cordon packed, Lara edged to MacGill, who juggled at fourth slip and held the chance.

The hat-trick ball was right in on Adams, a perfect, lifting delivery that committed him to play. He fended it off straight to Langer, who with some jubilation took the chance at short leg.

Extraordinarily, these were the only three wickets McGrath took in the innings, but in the process he achieved his 300th Test wicket, Lara's. In joining the elite list of players who've gone past 300, he was ranked sixth in the quickness of achieving it – 64 matches as against DK Lillee's 56. It was the first Australian hat-trick taken in Perth since Merv Hughes over 10 years earlier.

The West Indies in the end did well to make 196, with Ridley Jacobs playing the counter-attacking innings of 96 not out, and Wavell Hinds making 50 before he was almost casually caught by Mark Waugh at slip. They were all out about half-an-hour after tea.

For the West Indies, things went from bad to worse in the days that followed, and the match ended in a victory for Australia, their record-breaking 12th consecutive win. It was brilliantly achieved when Brett Lee took the last three wickets in one over.

He clean bowled McLean and Black; Courtney Walsh survived the hat-trick ball, but was plumb lbw to the last delivery of the over.

It triggered a wonderful Australian celebration and a rare hearing in public of the words of their victory song, "Under the Southern Cross I stand, a sprig of wattle in my hand."

Viv Richards went into the Australian dressing room to congratulate them on their record-breaking performance, a particularly appropriate act since he had been in the West Indies side in the 1980s that had set the benchmark of 11 in a row.

If the West Indies players were reeling by now, there was no respite, with the Third Test in Adelaide due to commence a little over a week later.

Their only consolation might have been that Steve Waugh was ruled out by injury – he had sustained a muscle strain in his buttock. At one point in the commentary I couldn't resist the opportunity to say, "Steve for some extraordinary reason in this period of success got a bum steer."

More than likely he'd be back in action for the following Test match in Melbourne, and it meant that Adam Gilchrist became the 41st Australian captain, and the first wicket-keeper to lead Australia since Barry Jarman in 1968. Although there had been very few captain/wicket-keepers in the history of Test cricket, recently it had become something of a fashion, with Alec Stewart having led England, Andy Flower captaining Zimbabwe, and at the present time Moin Khan the captain of Pakistan.

For the first time on tour the West Indies management was, almost, talking up their chances going into the Adelaide Test. Lara had at last found form, smashing 231 against Australia "A" in Hobart.

Curiously, and perhaps irrelevantly, his innings coincided with the return to England of girlfriend Lynnsey Ward. And in the Australian camp several

Yes, Prime Minister

THERE'S A LONG TRADITION OF VISITING DIGNITARIES IN THE ABC COMMENTARY BOX. SOME OF THEM KNOW, AND CARE, MORE ABOUT THE CRICKET THAN OTHERS.

It's hard to compare today's broadcasts with those of earlier times. I'd like to think there's still character in what we do today, and in a number of ways I think the product's better actually — we certainly get more out of the expert talent. Where it's a conversational style nowadays, then it was far more formal.

When I started commentating it was more or less a formula — you described the over and brought the expert in at the end of it. There wasn't a lot of conversation, and there was more stiffness about it than there is now.

Today we talk about so many different issues, not just the game as it's happening out there, and that's why we're fortunate to have expert commentators like Peter Roebuck, Geoff Lawson, Keith Stackpole, Bob Massie, Terry Alderman, Terry Jenner, all these chaps who work with us and know their game.

The technique is to draw them out and that's easier said than done. The same goes injuries had the potential to upset a winning rhythm.

In addition to Steve Waugh's buttock strain, Brett Lee had suffered a recurrence of a lower back strain, and, as a precaution, was rested. Australia plumped for spin in Lee's absence, calling on Colin Miller, who'd linked up with MacGill when Australia won the deciding Test in Antigua in 1999.

Damien Martyn, the long suffering attendant in waiting, replaced Waugh. For the West Indies 19-year-old Marlon Samuels, Chanderpaul's replacement, made his debut on the back of seven first-class matches, joining a growing list of young West Indian debutants.

Lara's appearance at last heralded what the crowd had hoped to see. After early wickets had fallen, he began sedately enough, knocked awry by a McGrath

for the famous guests who from time to deign to pay a visit.

When John Hewson was made the new leader of the Opposition after rolling Andrew Peacock in the early '90s, the party spin doctors decided to do some work on developing his public image.

One of their ideas was that, as had often been the case with the Prime Minister during Bob Hawke's time, he should make a guest appearance in the ABC box and also in the Channel Nine box during the Test match.

Brisbane was the chosen setting – it was the First Test of 1994-95 – and as I was the person on air at the time I'd had warning that he was going to pay us a visit. I hadn't met John Hewson before and there hadn't

been much information forthcoming from his minders, so I wasn't too sure what tack to take.

As luck would have it, as he came into the box, I looked away to the scoreboard and there happened to be two English names up there – English fast bowlers Devon Malcolm and Angus Fraser.

As Hewson sat down I said, "It's a delight to welcome the new leader of the Federal Opposition. Nice having you here today, Mr Hewson."

Then I said, "It must feel like old home week being here at the 'Gabba when you look at the scoreboard and you see Malcolm Fraser up there."

It was only then that I realised how nervous he was. He was sweating as he sat bouncer that zeroed in on his helmet. But he soon hit his stride, lambasting MacGill's underpitched deliveries.

His only blemish was a sharp chance that only Mark Waugh could have taken from MacGill's googly at slip; he didn't.

Lara found second-day support from new boy Samuels, who, in the manner of all talented novices, had that extra split second to adjust, and play late. Another double hundred loomed when Lara finally fell to Miller's off-stump spin, and a touch of extragance. Mark Waugh didn't miss a second time.

The rest was as predictable as another wedding party arriving on Saturday arvo in the adjacent parklands. Miller took the last five wickets for a collective 37 runs; 391 was competitive, but could Lara repeat in the second innings?

Meanwhile Slater and Hayden reminded us how well they can score on a true pitch when the bowling tends to be too attacking. They whistled past 150 in even time. A run-out reawakened the West Indies, and before too long Australia's chances of equalling the West Indies total looked remote. Mark Waugh and Ponting changed that with a fine partnership, which

down and my opening comment, meant to be light-hearted, seemed to throw him completely off balance.

He said something uncomfortably brief, and after that the conversation about the cricket staggered along. He seemed totally out of place, our talk agony for him.

Perhaps he did have some interest in the game, but it certainly didn't come out the way it does with John Howard, for instance.

He is a genuine cricket-lover – a "tragic" as Mark Taylor memorably said – and with him in the box you don't feel as if it's just a politician taking advantage of an opportunity. He was sitting with Kerry

O'Keeffe during one of the Australia v West Indies Test matches when Kerry remarked that he had a video tape at home featuring all the leading politicians playing cricket.

"Biomechanically," he said to Howard, "you've got the best off-spinning action I've ever seen from a politician." It was a wonderful line to feed a Prime Minister.

Howard always comes over well when he's in the commentary box, and Bob Hawke was the same. He had a pretty good knowledge of the game.

Neither Gough Whitlam nor Malcolm Fraser were interested in sport so it was Hawke who revived the Prime Minister's XI game after Fraser.

hepled their team top 400 and lead by a handful of runs on the first innings.

The tension of a close contest snapped on the fourth morning when Lara and Ganga were building a partnership from the disappointment of two early wickets, but a quicker Miller delivery clipped Lara's inside edge to pad, and Langer's short leg celebration was understandable.

The rest of the batting capitulated, Miller taking five for eight in 52 balls, as the West Indies folded for 141, losing eight for 54. Miller's second five-wicket haul meant that Australia required only 130 to win.

On a pitch that was starting to produce some variable bounce, the veteran Walsh charged in, supported by a fiery Dillon. Three catches to Jacobs, and a Ponting lbw, and Australia looked wobbly, without the steely presence of Steve Waugh.

I once got him to describe play in 1988-89 in the Second Test in Perth, which turned out to be an historic occasion for Merv Hughes.

I said, "Look, you've been here a few times and it's always a delight to have you along to talk about the game – perhaps you'd like to fill the role of the ball-by-ball commentator. Would you like a go?"

There was pause, then Hawkie said in his usual rasping way, "Oh, all right, I'll give it a go," and he started off, fumbling his way in a little at first.

He didn't quite get out that Merv Hughes was bowling ... what he did do was react to the immediate fall of a wicket.

"Oh, he's caught! He's out!"

Of course, Hawkie made a joke of it, saying that his value to the Australian cricket team would have improved immeasurably with this wicket that he'd taken "with my first ball".

As it turned out, it was the first ball of Hughes's hat-trick, the most amazing broken hat-trick ever taken.

This first wicket was with the last ball of an over. With the first ball of his next over he got the last wicket of the West Indies innings.

He'd got two wickets in two balls.

A day-and-a-half later, with the first ball of the West Indies second innings, he trapped Gordon Greenidge lbw, completing the hat-trick.

Beyond the "golden age"

WHO'LL FOLLOW IN THE FOOTSTEPS OF TODAY'S TEAM?

You've got to say this is the Golden Age of Australian cricket. Inevitably, following the team's record run of wins, many people start looking a little anxiously towards the future. In 10 years' time we may find ourselves looking back and saying, "Why can't we produce a team like that?"

Australia has got the structure and everything else to continue to produce good teams, but whether they'll have the quality of this particular side remains to be seen. You certainly don't see the quality of batting coming through at the moment as you did when Steve and Mark Waugh started their careers, and that is a worry for the future of Australian cricket.

"Are a lot of kids playing cricket?" we may ask. Yes, it seems to be the case.

"Are they getting the right grounding for the longer form of the game?" Yes, you can say there's plenty of opportunity.

So if we're asking the right questions, and these aren't the right answers, what's the problem?

There may be an argument that some youngsters are being over-coached, that their natural flair for the game is somehow lost in the process. Or that established players are staying in the game longer, so fewer good young players are given the opportunity to develop.

It's an attitude thing too. Perhaps they're not hungry enough. Perhaps they reach a comfort zone too early in their careers. It's a bit like some of the golfers in the US PGA tour — they go around week in and week out, hardly ever winning a tournament, but as long as they get the occasional top-10 finish they know they're going to get their tour card for the next year.

You've got to have that hunger to go to the next level and be a winner. Maybe we've featherbedded our cricket by having a second-tier level of professionalism in which everyone's paid to play first-class cricket.

You wonder how much toughness there is in the game at the moment. You've got to have the desire.

I remember talking to Wes Hall on his most recent visit to Australia. The great West Indian fast bowler is now the Reverend Wesley Hall, and I asked him if he was preaching to many congregations while he was here.

My question was greeted with a half-smile.

"You don't get many congregations in an affluent society," he said.

It's true. I don't know if you can make some parallel between cricket and religion, but too much affluence may have an effect on both.

Say so... *on his injury ... " It'll be hard to watch on TV, I'm sure.*
But I don't want to be hanging around when someone else has got the job of
being captain. I want to give that guy his freedom. " **Steve Waugh**

Langer dug deep, and with the composed Martyn,
helped to carry the innings to five for 98 at stumps. The
West Indies lacked the bowling variety, and next day a
flurry of shots ended in an embrace between Martyn
and stand-in captain Gilchrist.

Australia won by five wickets, a match that
Gilchrist described as the hardest of his career.

Australia's thirteenth straight Test win had clinched
the Frank Worrell Trophy.

The biggest day of the Test year in Australia is Boxing
Day. It's the day when there's the biggest turnout to
watch what normally is the highlight of a series.
Traditions die hard, and despite the fact that Australia
led 3-nil and had already won the series, the crowds
duly turned up for this occasion. There were 73,233.

Steve Waugh returned to the scene of his Test debut
in 1985. While recovering from his injury, and musing
over Australia's performances, Waugh had come to the
conclusion that the nightwatchman policy should be
abandoned. Australia had used stopgaps in the first
three Tests. Waugh's decision was another example of
challenging orthodoxies; why continue to do something
just for the sake of doing it?

Waugh's return meant that poor old Damien
Martyn was again on the sidelines. The chastened West
Indies introduced Guyanese fast bowler Colin Stuart,
who replaced Marlon Black. MacGill, who'd taken
some licks from Lara in Adelaide, made way for Andy
Bichel. Local knowledge suggested that seam and pace
bowling was more effective than spin at the MCG.

The day was warmed up by a tribute to Shane

Warne. Facing the crowd at the Richmond end, he was presented with a trophy that featured the ball with which he took his 356th wicket in Auckland in March. In the spirit of Boxing Day's festive celebratory mood, the large crowd watched Warne's moment, and later a lunchtime motorcade showing off every surviving Victorian-born Test cricketer. Young fans would have struggled to put names to some of the ancient faces, like George Thoms, who played one Test against the West Indies in 1951-52, but the vaudevillian Merv Hughes and his whiskers didn't require an introduction.

Australia batted after the West Indies won the toss, and they should have got rid of Slater early on – he was badly missed off Dillon by Campbell in the slips. As a result Australia got as far as 41 before losing their first wicket - which gave Courtney Walsh his 491st Test wicket. Australia really struggled in the early sessions to build some kind of a total. That eventually came with the doughty batting of Steve Waugh, who after Gilchrist had hung about for his 37-run share of a partnership of 61, found Gillespie – a perennial favourite in the tail – to play straight and to play sensibly. He batted for an

Say so... "*We're lucky we've had so many great times together. Some other sides don't get to experience any of those highlights. We've had probably 10 or 15 over the last 10 years.*" **Steve Waugh**

hour-and-a-half and they put on a good partnership of 70 before the close of play on the first day.

At 7-295, with Waugh on 98, Australia went into the second day in a strong position, and by the end of it had really buried the West Indies again. Steve duly went on to his 23rd Test century, and Australia finished at 364 with some good slogging in the tail from Colin Miller, to make 29. Even McGrath hung about for a little while and Steve Waugh was undefeated on 121.

Exploiting the pitch's bounce and movement, Gillespie and Bichel aimed consistently at the off stump. The result: 90 minutes of carnage. Ganga nicked one, so did Hinds, Lara, and Adams, while Campbell prodded Miller's off-spin to silly point. At 5-28 the innings was headed for oblivion. The exciting Samuels showed the temperament, and Jacobs the natural dogfight resilience to resuscitate the corpse. A one-handed Mark Waugh screamer in the slips removed Jacobs for 42, and when Walsh arrived after another Bichel/Gillespie blitz on the tail, eight runs were required to avoid the follow on.

The way the West Indies achieved it was pure Keystone Cops. They were nine wickets down, Courtney Walsh was batting, and he hit the ball away through the offside, achieving the two runs required to avoid the follow-on. Then, suicidally, he attempted a third and was run out. I'll never forget the sight of Courtney Walsh trying for that third run, legs and bat flailing about like an octopus.

So Australia had to bat again, which they did well enough to build up a position on the third day where they could make a declaration near the close at 5-262.

The Prince and the Moon

Among our celebrity guests, we haven't got as far as getting the Queen or Prince Philip as guests into the box, but I have met Prince Philip. He's the 12th man for the Lord's Taverners and has been their patron for a long time. I met him at a dinner when he was out here for the Bicentennial celebrations in 1988.

He "did" the room and when he came to our group I asked him about his interest in cricket.

I think Richie Benaud once saw him in action in the nets somewhere and said he had potential with his wrist-spin bowling. But I don't think the prince ever aspired to being a cricketer. He said he was into "carriages" rather than cricket – a bizarre sport and a good one for the somewhat rich.

Still, he was friendly and seemed interested in us.

He did make one odd remark.

"In all the time I've been on this trip to Australia," he said, "I haven't seen the moon once."

At that moment someone drew the curtains back and we looked outside and there was the moon. Prince Philip seemed very taken that someone should have bothered. It was weird.

And it did make you wonder how members of royalty occupy their time.

Justin Langer at last got some runs, and Mark Waugh a polished 78 not out, and they left the West Indies a target of 462 to win the game.

With 11 overs to get through – and two more days to play – by stumps the visitors' second innings was wrecked. They were 3-10. Gillespie hit Ganga on the pads, had Hinds caught at fourth slip, and bowled Lara without offer.

Lara's off stump uncertainty had bedevilled him, as he tried to cope with the relentless attack on his outside edge. The "knowing when to leave" policy is always dangerous against the moving missile, and Lara's duck chalked up an ignominious 24th for his team in the series.

Gillespie mowed down three more victims the next morning, and at six for 23, another all-time low was likely. Samuels batted defiantly again, his composure lasting until three-quarters of an hour after lunch. Then, running out of partners, he skied to Gillespie off Miller and Australia had prevailed by 352 runs.

Steve Waugh said the West Indies inexperience reminded him of Australia's plight in 1985. He noted that the West Indies had recently won the Under-15 World Cup, and that fresh faces like Marlon Samuels pointed to a brighter future.

Four down and one to play, that prospect seemed as distant as Australia winning soccer's World Cup.

It was hard to believe going into the Fifth Test in Sydney that things would change. The occasion was billed as the Centenary of Federation Test match, celebrating the birth of the Australian nation on January 1st, 1901.

Cricket's influence on that late-nineteenth century sense of nationhood had been a powerful unifying force. Long before the beginnings of national structures in government, industry and politics, cricket created the cooperation between colonies that led to England's recognition of a team that called itself Australia.

Say so... *"Steve Waugh commented on the young talent, and pointed to the bright future that beckoned for the West Indies. Four down and one to play, that prospect seemed as distant as Australia winning soccer's World Cup."*

Spectators who watched those early Test matches thought of themselves as Australians, even though, by law, they were resident British citizens.

In January 2001, recognising the significance of the moment, the Centenary organisers created special caps and commemorative coins for presentation to the Australian players at the start of the match.

The Sydney Cricket Ground had played a prominent role in the Federation festivities 100 years earlier. Banked by a sloping cycling track, the ground had hosted exhibitions of baseball, lacrosse, maypole dancing, ball throwing contests, and a Sheffield Shield match between NSW and South Australia. NSW compiled a record 918 to win by an innings, five batsmen scoring centuries.

A century on, and the new millennium Sydney Cricket Ground had been revamped especially for this occasion. New seats, new turf and a relaid pitch awaited the fans and the combatants.

An hour after lunch on the opening day, watched by a crowd of 40,880, the West Indies were 0-147, and Australia were looking ragged. New Year hangover, or simply a West Indies resolution to hit de ball, man?

Campbell, who'd been in out-of-season hibernation for two months, attacked. His new opening partner, Wavell Hinds, responded excitedly, and with Lara to come, 400 beckoned. Cue local hero Stuart MacGill, who hadn't played since Adelaide. Campbell sent him a dolly catch, Hinds played over a floater, and after making an impressive 35, Lara departed to another swift pick-up by Mark Waugh at slip.

In a restatement of old-fashioned values, the slip fielder's nod confirmed to Lara that he had made a fair catch – in two fingers and a left thumb, along the turf. Lara accepted it. No technology required.

Subsequently, MacGill, like a python entwining its prey, devoured the rest. In a whirl of bat, pads, lbws and a lightning Gilchrist stumping, the West Indies were nine for 256 at stumps.

Courtney Walsh couldn't stop laughing. He was about to face Colin Miller at the start of the second day when he noticed that Miller had gone blue.

Miller's number two haircut had been rinsed overnight in a "Federation" blue, and Walsh's paroxysm invoked laughter from the crowd. Walsh was probably still cackling when Hayden caught him off Miller at silly point.

Hayden's celebration was shortlived when, as Australia made an awkward start to its innings, the indefatigable Walsh quickly had him snaffled up by Lara at slip. Wicket number 493 on Walsh's steadying climb to that landmark 500th.

Slater got going belligerently, and after running out

Say so... *"Courtney Walsh couldn't stop laughing. He was about to face Colin Miller at the start of the second day when he noticed that overnight Miller's hair had gone a lurid shade of 'Federation' blue."*

Mark Waugh through a terrible call and mind-change, tried to get to his hundred with another big boundary. Premeditation and/or nervous nineties, he became the first player to be dismissed nine times in the nineties.

It cast an interesting sidelight on Michael Slater's state of mind, because that very morning before play began I had been the MC for a fund-raising breakfast put on by Sydney's Western Suburbs Cricket Club and the University of NSW. Slater had been a special guest. I had talked to him then about his propensity for getting out in the 90s, and he had responded in a very positive fashion to my questions. Perhaps he was in some denial over the problem – within a couple of hours he had a crack at a ball that wasn't on a length from top-spinner Nagamootoo and skied it straight out to Samuels in the covers.

He was on his way back for 96. It had looked like he had a hundred in the bank, then came that error of judgment, that rush of blood. It was further evidence, I thought, that at times this wonderful player does have brain explosions, and serious losses of judgment.

Steve Waugh and Ponting ensured an Australian lead. Gilchrist, dropped from his first ball edging straight to Adams in the gully, turned on the licks. Nagamootoo was the best West Indies bowler, but not even his variation and bounce threatened Gilchrist's savagery. Waugh's 24th hundred and Miller's innovative swats took the lead to 180.

Gilchrist's arrival on the third morning had coincided with Prime Minister John Howard's appearance in the commentary box. I had a bit of innocent fun by asking him if he'd give us a comment

Colin Miller: individualist

Miller To The Max

In spite of the pressures, today's players are probably no less individualists than the players of years ago. Colin Miller, for instance, is one player who hasn't been steeped in the Aussie team culture.

The world of professional cricket is a cosseted one. As a top player, there's always someone to pick up after you, so that basically all you need to concentrate on is getting yourself right to play cricket.

In the Australian team, you've probably been there for a long while and came into it a fairly early age.

In contrast Miller is a johnny-come-lately. He didn't play for Australia until he was 34 by which time he'd had a lot of experience of life outside cricket. He came into the Australian side with the maturity of a man who had travelled the world, worked in pubs, played cricket in England and Holland. So he brought a very different flavour to it.

On the field, too, he learnt a lot in a short time. A medium/medium fast swing and cut bowler for years, all of a sudden he decided that this off-spin thing was worth trying out. He was so successful he basically forced the selectors' hand – they couldn't ignore him after he got 67 Shield wickets in one season.

on GST. He looked at me quizzically, a little nonplused by a politically motivated question.

"You know, GST," I said keeping a straight face. "Gilchrist scores tons."

The West Indies again made another very good start and were 1-98 at the end of the fourth day. They were going along serenely when Wavell Hinds, so keen to make sure he didn't foolishly lose his wicket just before stumps, allowed the penultimate delivery of the day to pass. It straightened off the pitch from McGrath and hit his off stump.

It was just the tonic Australia needed and they started to pick up quick wickets the next day – McGrath got Adams, Gillespie picked up Campbell and Samuels, and was on a hat-trick. Lara survived.

While Lara was at the crease we experienced one of those strange coincidences that happen from time to time in the commentary box.

Robert "Crash" Craddock from *The Daily Telegraph* was a guest and telling us and the listeners about the Australian Cricket Media Association's "Player of the Year" award. The recipient this year was Colin Miller – I think they had renamed it the young-at-heart cricketer of the year award.

Anyway, prior to the ceremonies at the Sydney Hilton, Crash was carrying a framed photograph of Miller's award in the lift when Colin Miller, unaware that he was to be the winner, hopped into the same lift. As he tried to hide the award from Colin, Crash Craddock dropped it and the glass went crashing through the lift shaft.

Craddock was in the midst of this story on the radio when Brian Lara went for a big hit from the bowling of MacGill, skied the ball down towards Miller at mid-on. You wouldn't want to know – just as Crash said the words "I dropped the photo," Miller dropped the catch.

He made amends when Gilchrist held an edge, and

Say so... *"Courtney Walsh came out for his final innings in Australia and was given not only a standing ovation, but a rare guard of honour from the Australian players. It was a great moment of sportsmanship."*

....

for once the tail wagged with Sarwan, and two left-handers, Jacobs and Nagamootoo, flailing freely.

Courtney Walsh, whose imminent retirement on the brink of 500 Test wickets was a topic of some conjecture, came out for his final innings in Australia and was given not only a standing ovation, but a rare guard of honour from the Australian players. It was a great moment of sportsmanship.

Set 171 to win, Australia's early decline to 3-46 included Walsh's 494th wicket. It was clear that the pinnacle would remain elusive, at least until his return to the West Indies. Aged 38, he had struggled for success on the tour, taking 11 wickets in five Tests.

Another Slater attack, charging and cutting and hooking, rushed Australia towards the target. Ponting hit the winning runs to complete the 5-nil whitewash. It the most entertaining match of the series.

In the awards wash-up, Steve Waugh won the Sir Garfield Sobers Award for most outstanding batsman, his twin brother Mark took the Joe Solomon Award for best fielder, and Jason Gillespie claimed the Alan Davidson Award for best bowler, with 20 wickets. McGrath's match figures of 10-27 in Brisbane won the Norm O'Neill Award for the outstanding performance.

These awards were inspired by the 1960-61 teams. In his admiration for Australia's play Jimmy Adams must have wondered when a West Indies team would again compete with their most formidable rivals.

The One Day series was something of an anticlimax. Everyone expected Australia to triumph and they did so without losing a game against the West Indies and

Zimbabwe. The most exciting game of the series was the last one against Zimbabwe in Perth. It was a matter of pride, since it was already decided that Australia and the West Indies would play in the Final.

Australia in their "rotation" policy opened with Martyn who made 144no in the total of 5-302, and at one stage it looked like Zimbabwe might run this down. Eventually, 15 were required off the last over.

Zimbabwean Douglas Marillier came out and played the most extraordinary spoon shots from McGrath, walking inside the line and flicking the ball down to long leg. It was an inventive tactic and he very nearly pulled off the win.

They ended up going down by one run, at 6-301. Marillier's improvisation lives longer in the memory than anything else that had happened in that match and probably the whole series.

There was one good banner at the ground:

Flowers ever blooming, (Andy and Grant Flower)
A record scoring week,
If we just had one good win, (Murray Goodwin)
We'd be on a winning streak. (Heath Streak)

....

Say so... "*That degenerate Shane Warne, he smokes, he drinks, he speaks to women and now, shock horror, he uses unthinkable language ... When will it stop?*" **Letter to the Editor**

....

Australia won the first of the Finals in a canter. They scored 9-253, and the West Indies were gunbarrelled for 119 in 39.2 overs. It was embarrassing.

In Melbourne, Mark Waugh made 173, his highest score and the highest by an Australia in a one-day game, and the Australian total of 6-338 was their highest in Australia, the highest by any team in this country, and 11 runs short of their best effort ever. The West Indies made a more cheerful reply with 299, but it was never really on as a contest.

It rang the curtain down before Australia headed off to India in just over a week's time.

Shame, Shane, Shame!

WHO'S TO BLAME IF WE HEAR MORE THAN WE SHOULD?

There was controversy during the series about utterances from Shane Warne, who was heard on-air to sledge the Zimbabwean batsman Stuart Carlisle during a match at the SCG. The stump microphone picked up his remarks and all the television viewers could hear him swearing. The "c" word, among others, featured. Remember, too, the infamous "can't throw, can't bowl" remarks of "Joe the cameraman" were still fresh in people's memory from the previous season.

Now, to put it in perspective, as much as the players have to be aware of their responsibilities and some of the language is unnecessary, clearly the intrusion of the microphones and the monitoring of their output is an issue.

I don't think Carlisle, a fairly tough character with a thickish skin, was all that offended by the remarks. They were probably no worse than other cricketers might use when under a bit of pressure. But the fact that they were broadcast all around the country was a great disappointment. Warne did express regret that it reached the hearing of some viewers.

The incident prompted some amusing letters in the press

"Channel Nine should display a warning advising that the cricket is not suitable for children because of offensive language. When Shane Warne is playing perhaps it should show cricket only after 9.30."

"I see that ****** cameraman is back. Getting poor old Shane in trouble again."

"That degenerate Shane Warne, he smokes, he drinks, he speaks to women and now, shock horror, he uses unthinkable language in the course of top-level cricket. When will it stop? We simply can't have such people playing for Australia. Not only is it offensive to us Aussies but think of how disconcerting it must be to the opposition who have so graciously given up their time to play here and are no doubt decent, clean-living human beings.

"Now that the media coverage of these sportsmen and their cricket matches is so intense it's time for training of a different kind. Microphone technique should be de rigeur, coupled with elocution lessons so we at home can understand every word clearly and succinctly. Movement and deportment classes should be compulsory as those super-slo-mo sequences can be so revealing. Communication skills for relating to opposition teams in an orderly fashion should also be encouraged.

"For heaven's sake, why not choreograph the whole bloody match? Bring in a scriptwriter, a director and add a laugh track."

Mac

A TALENTED CRICKETER AND AN OBSESSIVE
STUDENT OF THE GAME, ALAN McGILVRAY
BROUGHT A LEVEL OF KNOWLEDGE TO HIS
RADIO COMMENTARIES THAT WAS UNEQUALLED.
OFF THE FIELD HE WAS UNEQUALLED TOO.

As I described earlier, Peter Meares was my first mentor as a cricket commentator, before I'd even got a job in the ABC, and his best advice can be summed up in a word: "Anticipate". The name Peter cited as his authority is a potent single word to budding commentators: "McGilvray". His daunting reputation has outlived him.

To come back to Peter's explanation of the main technique, anticipation. Let me give you an example. When the bowler runs in, instead of saying simultaneously, "Lillee comes in to bowl to Bradman," you say this *before* he bowls the ball. At the moment he delivers it you've set the action up so then you can continue the commentary and you're not beaten by the crowd. So ... "Lillee comes in" ... you're saying this as he runs in ... "and bowls" ... before he bowls ... "and Bradman goes back *and cuts* and Bradman's *caught at second slip.*"

This was something that later on I was able to refine, because I was working with Alan McGilvray, who was the master of the technique of cricket broadcasting. The absolute master.

The first match I ever did with him was New Zealand playing NSW. It was in December of the year I started and, given the way the ABC used to work in those days, I was fortunate to have the chance. Many of my contemporaries didn't get a chance to do anything more than "Sporting Highlights", our 6.30 programme every night from Monday to Friday.

The classic ABC experience was to be sent out to an outside broadcast to "observe" it. And there you'd sit, watching Norman May or McGilvray or whoever – some guys did this for ages, and weren't given a chance to broadcast an event for quite a while. I was fortunate to be thrown in at the deep end.

McGilvray was pretty intimidating as a personality. I can still picture the usual scene there in ABC Sport in the William Street offices down from Sydney's Kings Cross. Mac would be there, it would get to lunchtime and there'd be an adjournment to the Strand Hotel. This was where you learnt by listening.

Alan McGilvray made his first cricket commentary for the ABC about the time King Edward abdicated for the "woman I love", Mrs Simpson. At the same time a young Joe Louis was starting to show the form that made him the world's greatest fighter, and British shipbuilders were putting the finishing touches to the new superliner, *Queen Mary*. Essentially a cricketer first and a broadcaster second, McGilvray played for the NSW Sheffield Shield team in the 1930s, captaining the side in the summer of 1935-36. His life as a commentator for the ABC lasted 50 years and he was honoured by the award of the MBE in 1974 and the Order of Australia in 1980.

"You'll never be a broadcaster if you can't listen," McGilvray would say.

So you'd get into his company with Geoff Mahoney and the legendary all-rounder Norman May – there was quite a drinking contingent in the ABC in those days.

I've seen them drink a hell of a lot, mainly at the end of the day's play – I don't think I've ever seen any of what I'd call the legends of ABC sport in a condition where they couldn't broadcast.

But Mac was amazing, he used to drink throughout the day, and smoke too. He was certainly out of another era, a figure you couldn't imagine today. In these correct, healthier times, you'd have to go outside the ground if you wanted to have a cigarette, but Mac used to chainsmoke all day and go down to the bar after each 20-minute commentary stint. And his day used to start when we were on tour with "prayer meeting" in the hotel room – half-a-dozen bottles of beer consumed before you got down to the ground.

He must have had a pickled liver to be able to survive for as long as he did, on that kind of diet. But survive he did, and as I say, it didn't impair his

---

Say so... *on batting with Bradman in 1933 ...* "*40,000 people were there to see Bradman. Every time I was at strike, they were yelling, 'Get out of there and let Bradman have a go!'*" **Alan McGilvray**

---

performance. He was 75 or 76 when he retired, that's a long innings.

If you listen to the tapes of his broadcasts of the 1960s, the accuracy and sharpness of his delivery were extraordinary. He wasn't a great wordsmith, but he knew the game like no one else.

I still remember listening to the wireless as a kid when Australia were playing in England in 1964 and '68 in particular, and sweating on McGilvray to come back on the air.

Good as the other commentators were – Rex Alston, Brian Johnston, John Arlott and their colleagues had a lovely turn of phrase that was great to listen to – McGilvray always told you what was going on.

I think all of us in the ABC modelled ourselves on his style. I certainly did.

He used to say, "Copy technique not style, make your own style." He had the best broadcasting technique and probably the best Australian voice, too, that nice, soft, confidential, silvery tone. He analysed the game so well and was always authoritative.

As I said, he was intimidating for us, the budding apprentices. At one stage the ABC ran an advertising campaign using matchboxes with the slogan *The game's not the same without McGilvray* printed on them.

I recall one night in Mac's kitchen at his place in Double Bay, where we often used to go for a drink after a day's play, Lindsay Hassett pulling out a box of these matches and waving them at our host, stirring him up.

Mac flew into a rage.

"Who gave them permission?" he ranted. "Who gave them permission to create that thing? I certainly did not give them permission!"

There was a fair bit of "pompous maximus" about Mac in those days. He used to hold court in his Double Bay flat, pontificate I think is the word, and the stories would go on for hours.

He had a favourite trick. About 10 or 11 at night, with a lot of beer already drunk, he'd produce a bottle of "Black & White" whisky, flick the cork out of the

McGilvray's name will forever be associated with the audacious "synthetic" broadcasts which the then ABC sporting director, Charles Moses, contrived to cover the 1934 and 1938 tours of England.

"That remains the greatest experience I had in radio," McGilvray recalled. "We manufactured the commentaries from telegrams we received from England. Each over, we would get a cable which would tell us in code what happened to every ball. We had a picture of the ground in front of us, a scorer and a sound effects man. We made the sound of bat hitting ball by banging a pencil on a block of wood. In the end it almost felt like we were there."

One Expert to Another

Australian Prime Minister Sir Robert Menzies, of course, was an avid cricket fan, and he is famously recorded on tape giving McGilvray advice during a break in play at Lord's.

He spoke glowingly about the way McGilvray described the game in all its detail and excitement, and he offered him a word of advice ... "pausation" ... the dramatic pause. And, added the great public speaker, "Use the crowd."

McGilvray always liked telling the story of this conversation. It appealed to his self-esteem, I suspect.

The advice was probably superfluous, because Mac was doing exactly that anyway, he had such an instinctive feel for the game.

The Four Ms

....

DID MAC LIKE A DRINK? IS THE POPE A CATHOLIC?

Working on the commentary team with Alan McGilvray, I don't think a day went by in a Test match when you didn't have a drink. You had to be very, very ill not to. It was absolutely compulsory.

With Mac, at the end of the day's play we normally drank at the ground, retired to a hotel and ended up in his room. In Perth we used to go to a local pub opposite the ABC studios, the Carlton.

In Sydney he always used to go to the Lord Dudley in Paddington – there's now a commemorative plaque at his place by the bar. In Melbourne we used to have a few in the big Members Bar at the ground.

And there was a wonderful bar at the Windsor in Melbourne, as well as the Cricketers Club at the 'Gabba.

In Adelaide we stayed up at the Hotel Australia, North Adelaide, and used to drink in the bar there.

Does this sound like a non-stop pub crawl? It certainly was a defining part of your career. For me, going to lunch with McGilvray, Geoff Mahoney and Norman May became a fact of life – the three Ms became the four Ms.

Norman May used to broadcast on the weekends but during the week

> ### AT NOON NORMAN MAY WOULD TAKE TWO APC POWDERS. "THAT'S LUNCH," HE'D SAY, "LET'S GO AND HAVE A DRINK."

managerial decree said he had to spend time in the office. There wasn't much going on so he'd watch the traffic go up and down William Street all morning, waiting till it got to 12 o'clock. On the stroke of noon he'd open his desk drawer in his office, pull out two APC powders, throw them back and walk out to where we were sitting.

"I've had lunch," he'd say, "let's go and have a drink." And we'd all go down to the Strand Hotel.

John O'Reilly, a non-drinker, was one of our bosses in the ABC, and we used to take an audio tape with us so we'd have an alibi when we came back at half-past five to do "Sporting Highlights" at half-past six.

"Oh, I've just been up the road doing an interview, Mr O'Reilly."

This didn't happen every day, I might add, but one thing I can say – you became adept at sobering up for "Sporting Highlights".

Say so… on *Alan McGilvray's retirement from the ABC in 1985…*

" *It is difficult to nominate any one figure who has given so much pleasure to so many people over such a long period.* **" Bob Hawke**

kitchen window and put the bottle down.

"Right," he'd say, "no one's leaving until this is empty." We stuck it out. And you can bet we'd turn up the next day at the cricket feeling absolutely hopeless, struggling to get any words out at all.

Mac would get up in the morning, have bacon and eggs and toast and a couple of smokes, and he'd be right as rain. And this was when he was over 70. He was remarkable, just remarkable.

There are times in life when you get ahead of yourself. I made that mistake in 1983, when I got my first opportunity to do a cricket tour. It led to an unfortunate falling out with Alan McGilvray.

With the World Cup coming up in England that year, it was decided that I should go. There were people in the management of the ABC, including Derek White, who was then head of sport, who thought it was time to introduce someone else to the opportunity of covering major cricket.

Nevertheless, Mac was still the ABC's No 1 cricket broadcaster and quite obviously I was a relative junior. Mac had even said he didn't want to do all the tours any more, but the fact is he had always loved going on them and he wanted to have at least first refusal. After all, he had been, still was, the ABC's voice of cricket.

Also, as he got older and lonelier in his widowed state he became rather territorial.

At a function at the Cricketers Club of NSW someone asked me a question about this.

"Why is it, Jim, that you're going and not Alan McGilvray?" In hindsight, the answer I gave was a stupid one. What I *should* have said was that obviously Alan was delighted that someone was coming up through the ranks and had been given an opportunity and that he'd given me his full support – which would have been true.

Instead I made an offhand remark.

"Oh well, the ABC decided to send me and not Mac." It was as blunt as that.

I do have a habit, as my friends often remind me, of being a bit blunt about things if that's how I feel. It's a characteristic that can get you into trouble.

An account of what I'd said got back to Mac, and his hurt reaction proved what an insensitive, silly remark it had been.

In effect we had a falling out, and one that took a long while to repair. It wasn't till about 1988-89, some five years later, before the harmony was restored in our relationship. There was a degree of coolness for all that time, even after he retired in 1985, and it did make life difficult in the commentary box.

I can remember confiding to Keith Miller about it one day. I told him I didn't know how to handle the problem. What did he think I should do?

Keith used to phone McGilvray for a chat quite often – they even shared the same birthday – and he chose an opportune moment to bring it up.

"What's your problem with Maxwell?" he asked apparently, words to that effect.

To be honest, even today I don't know what the response was. What I do know is that as a result Mac eventually came round. I remember we were at the Cruising Yacht Club in Sydney one day for a reunion lunch with a number of people in and outside the ABC.

Mac broke the deadlock. After the lengthy period when there had been no communication and a distance between us, he commented to me that he thought the coverage of a recent series had been good. It was just a few simple, dignified words – but so gratifying to hear.

Our relationship became far more friendly after that, and lasted through the last seven or eight years of his life years until he died in 1996.

Zest for life

····························

LIKED BY EVERYBODY, KEITH MILLER IS UNIQUE.

I'll always be grateful for what Keith Miller did to help mend the bridges between Mac and me. As a player Keith was a magnetic personality and he carried that charisma into his years beyond the game. I worked with him in the '70s and '80s when he was involved in ABC television, and enjoyed his zest for life.

He never forgot anyone's name, for example. He had the same instinctive ability that some politicians have, and it probably helped make him such a popular figure in England. He was hale and hearty with everyone he met, from the top to the bottom, without a hint of snobbishness.

On the 1983 tour of England I went out one day with Keith to lunch, which turned into a long one. He was on the nod in about four pubs in London — he worked for the *Daily Express* for years, and his connections were amazing.

There's the famous story about him at a Test match at Lord's. Gary Sobers was in full flight one afternoon, batting for the West Indies, but Keith missed the action because he had spent the afternoon in a bar in the Members Pavilion from where you can't see the cricket. At teatime, people came rushing in.

"Did you see that fantastic innings?" someone said to Keith, who was deep in conversation. No reply.

"Did you see that six of Sobers, Keith?" the excited fan insisted.

Keith turned around slowly.

"Nope," he said, "didn't come in here."

Quite often, so the story goes, Keith would write his copy despite not having seen much of the day's play. He'd get an opinion from someone, ask a couple of pertinent questions, and write his piece on that. And his views would probably be as accurate as anyone else's, because of his intuitive knowledge of the game.

He had a casual air towards the business of broadcasting too. Quite often at the SCG during a Sheffield Shield match, he'd come into the box after tea and it would be clear that he hadn't seen a lot of the play.

He'd study the action for a few moments, eyeing up the batsman at the crease with due consideration. "This fellow looks as though he can play," he'd say, "where's he from?" And it was then that you might have to explain that it was Allan Border, and that he'd just made two or three hundreds.

Keith isn't as mobile as he used to be, but there's still that refreshing honesty about everything he does. He doesn't have airs or graces, and he doesn't hang back in his opinions. He is universally popular, and during the Ashes series and every English summer, he is a regular in a hospitality box at Lord's.

India

A TOUR OF INDIA IS HISTORICALLY ONE OF THE
MOST DIFFICULT ON THE INTERNATIONAL
CRICKET CIRCUIT. TIMES MAY HAVE CHANGED,
AND A FIVE-STAR WELCOME AWAITED THE
AUSTRALIAN TEAM IN FEBRUARY 2001, BUT THE
ENORMITY OF THE CHALLENGE REMAINED.

I flew out of Sydney on February 23, looking forward to my fourth visit to the subcontinent and a Test series that promised to make history. I was among the optimists who believed that a straight 3-0 victory might be achievable against India. Steve Waugh's unstoppable team had just notched up its record 15th Test win in a row and the chances of stretching it to 18 straight was definitely on, or so I thought.

Arriving in Mumbai, the coastal city that once upon a time everyone called Bombay, is an instant culture shock. Here, the relatively clean air and sedate streets of Australian cities are memories of another life; in their place is a world of traffic-induced smog and the staggering polarity of rich and poor in India.

We flew in at two in the morning, and in the brief period waiting for a car to pick us up at the terminal building, we saw a dozen people sleeping beneath blankets on the footpath. On the 40-minute drive through the warm night from the airport to the hotel, unfamiliar sights and sounds assailed the senses. Mumbai reveals life in all its amazing variety, from well-to-do sophisticates in a city where top real estate prices are even higher than New York's to entire families living, working and sleeping on the streets.

Mentally, I had prepared myself, together with Glenn Mitchell and my colleagues on the ABC Radio team, for the usual frustrations of organising the broadcast. We were scheduled to provide ball-by-ball commentary of each Test, a job that I knew would be a challenge. In India everyone is delighted to help but, to borrow a phrase, they do things differently there.

Still, I thought, as I checked into the Mumbai Oberoi Towers Hotel, I was ready for anything.

Except what actually happened.

"Bradman is dead."
February 26, 2001 ... a remarkable day ... the death of a legend. I was wakened by the phone ringing in my hotel room at two o'clock in the morning. It was the

Prior to the three-Test 2001 tour Australia had not won a Test series in India since 1969-70 when Bill Lawry led the tourists to a 3-1 win with one draw. Match results overall since Tests began between the two countries in 1947 were:
Tests: 57;
Wins: Australia 28, India 11;
Draws: 17;
Ties: 1.
Of the 29 Tests played on the subcontinent, Australia had won nine, India seven, with 12 draws and one tie.

ABC in Sydney with the news that Sir Donald Bradman had died peacefully in his sleep, age 92, the day before, on Sunday morning. The ABC had been one of the first with the news of Bradman's demise and the circumstances of his passing. I was still half asleep and my brain moved fairly slowly as I was asked if I could come up with a two-minute piece for radio encompassing the major features of his life. I pointed out that there was already a three-minute tribute on file in the Sydney studios, with actuality, that I had recorded some time ago for exactly this purpose. But no, that wouldn't do – they wanted something fresh.

And so, within an hour or two of hearing the news, I provided the last item in a little package for ABC Radio's "AM" programme highlighting his career. The Prime Minister, John Howard, who was in New Zealand, spoke with some affection and knowledge of Bradman, whom he had seen a week or two before his death. Howard reported that he had been in ill health and had gone into hospital with pneumonia in December. Following the Prime Minister there was a short piece from Bill Brown, one of Bradman's team-

Say so... "*We got lots of messages from Australia and everyone told us to carry on and play good cricket. We thought the best way to show respect to Sir Don was play top-quality Test cricket.*" **Steve Waugh**

mates from the 1948 side. Then it was my turn.

I attempted to cover just a little of his life and to make some comparative analysis of his place alongside other great sporting heroes of the 20th century. Purely on the raw statistics there's no doubting Bradman's dominance in his own sport. He was a phenomenon.

Consider the fact that he scored 6996 runs at an average of 99.94, while any other of the great players before or after him only managed to average in the low 60s. We're talking about a 60 per cent difference between Sir Donald Bradman and the lesser mortals, and that means every other fine batsman in the history of the game. On those statistics alone Bradman stands supreme. Add to that the fact that he scored a hundred on every third visit to the crease. It was really only Bodyline that brought him down. Even then he averaged what most would consider very good numbers, over 56 in the series, when England tried to come up with a tactic that would unseat him after his amazing series in England in 1930 when he scored 974.

I was not asked, nor did I give, my own personal experiences of Bradman. Just as well, because curiously enough, in spite of my involvement in cricket as an employee of the ABC since 1973, I never met him.

The opportunity may have come up once or twice, but it seems to me he was one of those figures respected from afar. The closest I might have got to him was standing next to him in the toilets at the SCG when I was a kid of 10 or 11. Growing up mad about cricket, I often sat across the aisle from him at the same ground. Bradman, Dudley Seddon and Jack Ryder, who were the three national selectors, used to sit always in the same designated pew in front of the ABC box.

The only other time I got close to meeting him was when I went to see a stockbroker years ago, before I worked for the ABC, when I was about 20, choosing to throw my money around during the Poseidon boom.

And there was the Don in the waiting room. As I recall, he was a director of a couple of public companies, but I don't know why he was there at Rene Rivkin's firm. I thought for a moment, should I say, "I'm Jim Maxwell," but it didn't happen.

So I never met him. My memory of him is that he had such an icon status you'd have been more likely to bowl up to the Prime Minister than Don Bradman and introduce yourself. He was a world apart.

As soon as I finished the discussion on "AM" about Bradman's place in the pantheon, I made an early-morning run from the Oberoi down to the Taj Mahal Hotel, where both the Australian and the Indian teams

Bradman's batting style was memorably summed up by Australian cricketer Jack Fingleton: "He loved the crash of the ball against the boundary fence; he delighted in seeing the figures revolve against his name on the scoreboard; he loved to murder bowlers and make the opposing skipper look foolish. There were, as I have written, no deft passes or pretty glides, but every bowler, every fieldsman, every spectator in Bradman's heyday sensed he was not using a bat so much as an axe dripping with the bowler's blood and agony. He knew no pity; he was remorseless."

The batting averages were:

	First class	Tests
Matches	234	52
Innings	338	80
Not outs	43	10
Runs	28,067	6996
Highest	452*	334
50s	69	13
100s	117	29
Average	95.14	99.94

What's the score, Mr Subramanian?

....

DID HE EVEN EXIST? JIM RECALLS A UNIQUE SCORER

In 1998 when we were in Chennai at the First Test I was asked if we needed
a scorer, and that was how we met Mr Subramanian. He turned up with his big
scorebook like all scorers and, as it transpired, he had a certain way about him. I'll
never forget his disembodied voice on that tour when Australia were getting dusted.
Me: "What are the details of Slater's innings?"
Mr Subramanian: "Fifteen minutes, fourteen balls, No-o-o-o-ooo boundaries."
The relish with which he used to deliver "no boundaries" cut us up every time. And
the look on his face, he was loving it; schadenfreude.
He became part of the furniture after that Test and we thought we'll pick someone
up some other place but he offered to travel, if we'd pay his train fare. He said he
had a relation in Calcutta, he could stay there, and in Bangalore, so we paid his
train fare and match fee. It wasn't a lot by Australian standards but a lot more than
All India Radio was paying. His
full-time job is as scorer for
Indian Cements, a big Indian
corporation. They have eight
cricket teams who play cricket
full time and these players are
only employed to play against

> "I WILL NATURALLY DISCHARGE
> MY DUTIES TO YOUR
> SATISFACTION ... OR MEET
> YOU AS YOU MAY DESIRE."

other big companies such as Indian Pistons, Indian Bank and so on. It's a carry-
on from the days of the maharajas, old-fashioned patronage in the 21st century.
For 150 days a year Mr Subramanian scores for Indian Cements but since by late
February cricket was moving out of the main season, he was free to work with us.
He wrote the ABC a letter before the Indian tour offering his services. I feel sure
he won't mind my sharing his words:
"I take the liberty of writing to you, as one who has had the privilege of being your
official scorer for the Australia-India tour of 1998. I sincerely hope you
remember me. May I approach you again to offer my services to you for the
forthcoming season. I would consider it a great honour to be associated with you
and to take care of this area. Since you have already had an occasion to evaluate my
services, I am sure you will be good enough to give me the opportunity again. I will
naturally discharge my duties to your satisfaction. I would greatly appreciate your
dropping me a line, so that I am get ready (sic) for the assignment, or meet you
with a prior appointment as you may desire."
I did desire. Mr Subramanian's offer was irresistible.

Say so... "*I really hope that people won't enshrine my dad too much. This iconic stuff is a little bit troubling. They should see him and reflect on the qualities that make people feel as they do.*" **John Bradman**

were staying. I needed to grab a couple of quick slices of wisdom, some reflection, from the key protagonists. Remember that though it may have been breakfast time in Sydney it was very early in Mumbai and so it meant making a few phone calls, one to the media liaison man with the Australian team, Brian Murgatroyd.

He had not heard the news from Australia and when I asked what he intended to do with the information he simply said that there would be a note placed under the door of each player.

As it transpired, by the time I got down to the Taj Mahal around eight o'clock in the morning a number of players had had phone calls from radio stations in Australia and some of their wives had also called with the news. The phones kept going throughout the morning right up to the time we got down to do that chat with the players.

I could see that they were moved and affected.

Steve Waugh spoke in a statesmanlike fashion about Bradman's influence and the personal inspiration that he felt he had had on all Australian cricketers, including himself. Handling himself extremely well as ever, he touched on Bradman's ability to unite the country during the Great Depression of the 1930s, when Australia was still striving for a sense of nationhood. He also spoke very fondly of the one-and-a half-hour meeting he'd had some years ago, his only ever opportunity for a one-on-one discussion.

But probably the most important remarks Steve made related to the question of whether or not he felt Bradman's death on the eve of the important First Test match would unify the side in their cause to win for the first time in 31 years in India. He took a very wide and international view of this. It was a wake-up call to

The unforgettable Mr Subramanian, whose "disembodied voice" some people thought didn't really exist. Some listeners thought we were doing him down – why were we making Mr Subramanian travel by train, they demanded to know, when we all flew? They thought that was being particularly mean of the ABC. I had to explain the nature of our arrangement (see box, opposite). As the series progressed, Mr Subramanian even had his own fan club in Australia.

I was in Calcutta when I got a call from the executive producer of ABC Television in Adelaide. Would I be interested in doing the commentary at the cathedral? Well, you don't get too many chances to do a memorial service for Sir Donald Bradman...

everyone about the future of the game, he said, because Bradman had played the game for the right reasons. Bradman represented the true values of the game and not just the selfish interests of those people who play for themselves – which of course was one of the reasons why the game in recent times had fallen into such disrepute. Among the corps of battle-hardened broadcasters and journalists who heard those sentiments that morning, I doubt if any one of us would have disagreed with a single word.

Shane Warne spoke of his meeting with Bradman on the occasion of his 90th birthday when he had accompanied Sachin Tendulkar out to his house in Adelaide. Tendulkar, India's inspirational batsman, wanted to speak too. He recalled that "very special moment" in Adelaide and revealed that he had framed photographs of Bradman, himself and Shane Warne set to go into his new house. In the last few years of his life Bradman had made the observation that he saw in Tendulkar some of himself – the highest compliment that a player like Sachin Tendulkar could receive.

Justin Langer said that he had already had a number of Indian friends call him to express their enormous sense of loss, not only because they held Bradman in such high regard but because with his passing the opportunity to meet him was gone for ever. They felt the loss in a profound way.

Sitting back and thinking about it later, it was all quite curious in a way. Here was a man who had lived for nearly 93 years, who had really played out the best cricket of his life some 53 years ago and beyond. It was hard to believe that he could still hold the public gaze. All these years on, almost a lifetime in some parts of the world, it seemed extraordinary that he should be so cherished and idolised.

Yet that's how it was, and the extent of it was brought home to me when I was given the chance to play my own small part in the memorial service at Adelaide's St

Peter's Cathedral some weeks later. During the Second Test in Calcutta, I got a phone call from Margot Phillipson, the executive producer of television in Adelaide, who told me the ABC were going to be covering the service live and would I be interested in doing some commentary? Well, you don't get too many chances to do a memorial service for Sir Donald Bradman, so I said sure, it's nice to be asked.

I knew Tim Lane was doing it on the radio, a pretty tough assignment for him because it would need far more embellishment than television.

An interesting aspect to this event involved the choice of colleague I was to work with, and the furore it created. Margot Phillipson asked me who I thought would be a good person to have alongside me doing the

There was no love lost between Don Bradman and his team-mate Test spinner Bill O'Reilly (see box overleaf). But O'Reilly could be generous: "There's never been and never will be in my estimation a batsman as good as that fellow. I don't care how many you like to pour into one – all the Chappells, the Borders and so on. Forget them, they're just child's play compared with Bradman, and I've seen them all. The Yanks talk about Babe Ruth and all that. To hell with Babe Ruth. This boy was a modern miracle."

New Betting Scandal Revealed

I make it a mission that I like to have a bet. I hasten to add that I have no inside knowledge.

In Adelaide in the Australian summer, Brian Lara was going mad in the West Indies innings and I rang up a certain bookmaker (my friends will know who I'm talking about) and said what's the best price you can give me on Australia to win the game. The West Indies at this stage were over 400 and he said 5-2, so I said OK. On a two-horse race when you think it's an even-money chance, 5-2 is a good bet. My thinking was the West Indies can do this once but they can't do it twice. I went very close to doing my dough because Australia had to get some runs in the second innings to win the game and it got a bit ropey there for a moment, but Damien Martyn and Gilchrist made sure that Australia won. So I won my money. Confident of

Australia's ability, I rang up the bookmaker before the Indian series and said I wanted three quotes:

1. First Test. He gave me over the odds, 3-1 Australia, so I bet on that.
2. Two-nil, I was given 8-1, so I had a bet on that too.
3. Three-nil, 20-1, and I bet on that.

And you'd have to say after two days of the Calcutta Second Test, that I was in good shape. If only I'd known...

I should have gone back to Richie Benaud's old wisdom: "Don't bet on anything that can talk."

At least I draw the line at one-day cricket. I bet on Test matches because they're a genuine full assault on life, but in one-day games too many things can go awry.

As my old friend Peter Wilkins would say, I'm "an appalling judge of horse form." So I'm lucky to have got some of it back on the cricket.

commentary. I said it was difficult – how much commentary would there be for a start? – but I think Sam Loxton's name came up, the humorous and talkative man who was one of Bradman's colleagues in the legendary 1948 team.

It came as a surprise when the next thing I heard on the grapevine when I was in Chennai during the Third Test was that Tony Squires, journalist and presenter of the ABC's amusing half-hour programme "The Fat", was going to be used. But I quickly reasoned, having met Tony on "The Fat", that he'd make sure he didn't come out with any faux pas.

It was only when I got home that the extent of the negative reaction filtered through to me. Reporters and photographers from Sydney's *Daily Telegraph* had turned up at Tony's house asking if he intended to be irreverent and make light of what was a dignified occasion. People just thought he was the wrong choice. I gather that he even had to go down to Adelaide to do

Bradman: the other side

I THINK THERE'S A BIT OF BLINKERDOM IN CRITICISMS OF BRADMAN, BUT THEN I'M ONLY A THIRD PARTY. FOR WHAT THEY'RE WORTH, HERE ARE SOME DISSENTING VIEWS...

How do you rate Bradman?" I asked my fellow commentator Peter Roebuck while we were in the box together at the Test match in Mumbai. It was a couple of days after he'd died, and a topical question obviously.

"Well, I don't know why everyone's getting so carried away," Roebuck said. "He was a great cricketer but that's all he was. He wasn't like Learie Constantine or Sir Frank Worrell. These were great men who had a serious impact on society.

"All Bradman was was a great cricketer. That was it."

It was a typically blunt, unsentimental – you could never say Peter Roebuck's sentimental – response from Roebuck, and it made me think of other things I'd heard said of the Don over the years.

Ian Chappell never got on with Bradman, for instance. He was asked in India if he would make a comment after Bradman died and he refused point blank.

I think he took the view that if you can't say something nice about someone then don't say anything at all.

Chappell talks about various

a kind of kiss and make up with the Bradman family to ensure this didn't occur.

As it turned out, I thought Tony Squires did a good job. Whether or not he was the right choice, it is arguable. Karen Tighe would have been a good choice or even Kerry O'Brien, because it did need a kind of gravitas. It wasn't the sort of occasion at which you could be at all flippant.

Not that Tony was, he curbed his style to suit the event and I thought he did it very well.

As for my role in the proceedings, there wasn't much commentary needed because the service basically ran itself. I felt privileged to be there in the atmosphere

experiences during his captaincy career that made him feel less than warm towards Bradman. In the years leading up to the breakaway formation of World Series Cricket in 1977, the issue of player payments was a constant sticking point with Chappell and his team. Bradman appeared to be happy enough with players earning money because of their cricket profile and reputation, as he would have done, but when it came to rewarding them as

sporting professionals, there was a sense of jealousy, and even that Bradman would be parting with his own money.

Chappell detailed instances of Bradman's reluctance to make better provisions for the players in "Chapelli: The Cutting Edge", published in 1992. Chappell described one of his meetings with the ACB, where he had followed Richie Benaud's advice about putting all the points he wanted to make in writing, as follows: "When it came my turn to speak on the points I had listed for each board member, I couldn't help noticing Sir Donald's reaction. He was sitting on my right a few seats away and for the first few points he sat back in his chair. When I came to the two matters on finance he sat forward listening intently. After I finished each point he explained in his distinctive tone, and in no uncertain terms, that the Board couldn't entertain such ideas. After

going into the Ashes series in England.

That remark hurt O'Reilly, who was subsequently disillusioned by Bradman's batting tactics in the Bodyline series, when "he tried to score as many runs as possible without being hit, tactics which were beyond the ability of his team-mates, and were damaging to team morale."

Bill told many stories from his front row observation deck in the old SCG press box when he was writing for the Fairfax

THE FIRST BARB WAS PROBABLY THROWN IN 1930 WHEN BRADMAN SUGGESTED THAT BILL O'REILLY WOULD NOT BE MUCH USE ON TURF, GOING INTO THE ASHES SERIES IN ENGLAND. IT WAS ONE OF SEVERAL ISSUES THAT RANKLED WITH O'REILLY FOREVER.

his little harangue, he sat back in his chair and had nothing more to say ...

"I think the policy of keeping match payments at a minimum contributed to the success World Series Cricket officials had when a couple of years later they approached Australian players with a contract."

For persistent animosity you'd be hard pressed to go past Bill O'Reilly. O'Reilly's relationship with Bradman began with their legendary meeting when Bowral played Wingelo in 1926 and Bradman took a double century from O'Reilly's team. O'Reilly respected Bradman as a player, but several issues rankled with him forever.

As told in Jack McHarg's authorised biography on O'Reilly, "A Cricketing Life", the first barb was probably thrown in 1930 when Bradman suggested that O'Reilly would not be much use on turf,

newspapers. The recurrent image of Bradman's aloofness, bordering on being anti-social, came across, and the subject of Clarrie Grimmett, O'Reilly's spin bowling mate, roused Bill's distemper.

The other major incident had its roots in the sectarian rivalry between Catholics and Protestants in pre-war Australia. O'Reilly and three other Catholic members of the Australian team were carpeted by the Board for allegedly not supporting Bradman during the 1936-37 series. Nothing came of the meeting, and Bradman denied that he had anything to do with it. The rift, more hostile on O'Reilly's side than Bradman's, persisted for the rest of their lives.

Sir Donald Bradman's reaction to the issues regarding O'Reilly's carpeting, and Grimmett's demise, have been the subject of much conjecture over the years. Correspondence exists between him and writer Jack McHarg, letters written in 1991 after the publication of McHarg's biography of O'Reilly. There had been fairly lurid, and somewhat inaccurate use in the press of material from the book. This publicity had upset Bradman, in particular a newspaper allegation that O'Reilly had "hated" Bradman.

When the McHarg letters are able to be published – unfortunately Bradman's executors declined our request for

he had been behind this disciplinary move is something that he is at pains to deny. That Bill refused to accept his word on this was plainly a cause of hurt.

On Clarrie Grimmett's omission, Bradman provides extensive and detailed statistical support debunking "O'Reilly's florid and unjustifiable claim" that Grimmett was discarded like an old boot.

In a later letter, Bradman's tone is even more emotional. He has given his

IN A LETTER TO O'REILLY'S BIOGRAPHER, BRADMAN'S TONE IS EVEN MORE EMOTIONAL. HE HAS GIVEN HIS ASSURANCE. IF THIS NOT ACCEPTED, THEN HE IS BEING CALLED A LIAR, AND THAT IS "THE HEART AND SOUL" OF THIS INCIDENT THAT HURT HIM SO MUCH.

permission to print them in full here – the record can be put straight, and best of all, in Bradman's own words.

There is no doubting the strength of his resentment. In his first letter, dated January 16, 1991, he makes it clear that it would be an understatement to say that he was upset by what had appeared in the press. He uses phrases such as "absolutely furious" and "legal advice", believing that he had been defamed. He alludes to the fact that he had waited before writing, fearing that had he committed his initial feelings to paper it might have destroyed their relationship for ever.

What rankled was that such allegations were the opposite of the truth as he saw it. "Bill may not love me," he wrote, "but certainly he has never hated me."

Regarding the episode when Catholic members of the Australian team had been carpeted by the Board, the allegation that

assurance. If this is not accepted unequivocally, then he is being called a liar, and that, he says, is "the heart and soul of this incident" which had hurt him so much.

By this stage, rightly or wrongly, Bradman had clearly had enough of the whole affair. It was "pretty nonsensical", he said, to raise it after over 50 years.

The final words on the rift come from O'Reilly. I remember sitting in the lunch room at the WACA ground in Perth and asking O'Reilly about his views on Bradman. "I can tell you respected him as a player, Bill," I said, "why don't you make some of your opinions public?"

He just looked at me across the table, sagely, seriously.

"Son," he said, "you've got to understand, history does not look favourably upon those that piss on monuments."

of the cathedral on such a day. It was one of those classic times in broadcasting when silence is golden.

The drama of Bradman's death aside, there was a lot for me and my ABC colleagues to do if we were to be ready for the action of the First Test. The coverage of the big story had left us with very little time to spare. At 9.30am the following day, the first ball of the series would be bowled.

In India, where everyone and everything can seem hell-bent on putting obstacles in your path, it's important to have professional, knowledgbable – and

Another, sometimes overlooked, aspect of Bradman's influence was brought home to me when my young son Hamish first went to the cricket at the SCG. He was puzzled.

"Daddy," he asked me, "why are they bowling from different ends?"

television rights. Back in the 1970s Packer couldn't get these rights because the ACB had a deal with the ABC, and no amount of money he put on the table – over a million dollars at the time – changed matters. The board stuck with the ABC. Kerry Packer is not a man who takes

KERRY PACKER WANTED THE RIGHTS TO THE CRICKET, BUT NO AMOUNT OF MONEY HE COULD PUT ON THE TABLE CHANGED MATTERS. HE IS NOT A MAN WHO TAKES KINDLY TO BEING DENIED WHAT HE WANTS...

He'd watched so much cricket on television he thought they always bowled from the same end.

It was a small but striking example of how cricket has been revolutionised by television. Of course one name will be forever linked to that fact: Kerry Packer.

To understand the Packer crisis you need to realise that basically it was about

kindly to being denied what he wants, and it was the way they treated him that upset him more than anything else. So he went off and started his own teams. The shockwaves through the game were personal, professional and financial.

What's sometimes forgotten is the role played as a peacemaker by Sir Donald Bradman. Packer is a businessman and adaptable – partners on the broadcasting team. It helps to have a mate, too, so I was particularly pleased to be joined on the team by my experienced Perth-based colleague Glenn Mitchell.

I've known Glenn for quite a few years, but this was the first time we'd been on tour together. Joining us from time to time in the box would be a number of experts, all old favourites with Australian fans: Peter Roebuck, Greg Matthews, Mike Coward and the voice and face of Indian media, Harsha Bhogle.

Curiously, from the time Alan McGilvray retired in 1985, the ABC has never appointed anyone as full-time cricket commentator. It's always been a bit of this, a bit of that. The attitude today is that Tim Lane and I

a pragmatist, and in a sense so was Bradman. The need was urgent. In the long term Packer wanted the television rights without the baggage of running the game, and for his part Bradman appreciated the benefits to cricket from what Packer could offer. After the war, it

BBC, used to cover it from one end only. Packer would have none of that, and said so with typical bluntness.

"Who wants to look at the arse of half a dozen players for half the game?"

Day/night cricket was another of his great innovations. In terms of what his

PACKER IS A BUSINESSMAN AND A PRAGMATIST AND IN A SENSE SO WAS BRADMAN. THE NEED WAS URGENT. BRADMAN REALISED THAT AND SO IT WAS HIS IMPRIMATUR THAT BROUGHT THE WARRING PARTIES TOGETHER.

was the endorsement of a peace agreement by Bradman and Packer that fixed things.

From that time on the ABC was no longer the national televiser of cricket. The money that Packer punched into the game was enormous, bringing innovations that today we take for granted, such as always covering the action from the bowler's end. Previously the ABC, like the

entrepreneurial vision and skill brought to the game you'd have to say it's all been positive. Bradman realised that, and in the end it was Bradman's imprimatur that made sure that World Series cricket and establishment cricket got back together again. That was the influence he had – not only as a player but as an administrator. People shouldn't forget that.

are the main established commentators and, basically in the interests of the credibility of the public, one or both of us does all the major tours. But that's not to say that that will always happen.

The fact that I've been editor of the "ABC Cricket Book" from 1988 and have been leading off the commentary for a longer period than anyone else, would lead some people to see me as the ABC cricket commentator. But the ABC, consciously or otherwise, has taken a view that it's not going to have an obvious No 1 cricket person. That's the way it has been, even during the self-ordained period of Neville Oliver's reign, and it suits the lifestyles of many of us too.

Take Glenn. He's married to ABC sports reporter Karen Tighe, and the demands of their careers make it necessary to manage the realities of a long distance relationship, as Glenn puts it. Being in the same trade helps, of course, but I know Glenn would have loved to have been in Adelaide with Karen that same day, when she was at the Sports Awards, and collected the well-deserved accolade of Media Personality of the Year.

Let's be honest, when you've got a family and you're away on tours all the time, it has the potential to ruin relationships. From my viewpoint it would be difficult if I were doing every tour. It's a wonderful experience, but it's more of a single man's existence. And it's not just in radio – the newspaper guys are now sharing the trips and working around the demands, so that each journalist can spend time with his family.

As I say, it's a great opportunity to see the world in all its variety. And the vagaries of Indian life notwithstanding, that morning it was Glenn's and my job to see that the set-up for the broadcast was in order.

In Australia, and many other parts of the world, you just walk into the commentary box knowing that everything is going to work. Not here. In India, as in Pakistan and to a lesser extent Sri Lanka, the broadcasters have to provide their own equipment. All we're given is a connection from the local phone company and we're left to put the broadcast together. Because nothing is straightforward in India, this creates

Say so... "*The crowds are going to be noisy and the wickets are probably going to be different. In times of need, we've got to stay calm and relaxed and composed. That will be crucial.*" **Steve Waugh**

its own series of frustrations and annoyances, and many promises of "man come, man be here soon."

It was late morning by the time we arrived at Wankhede Stadium, and the Australian players were packing up to leave after a short training session. Given the early start and the news of Bradman's passing, it had already been a long day for them. We had a brief chat with some of them, then made our way up to the commentary position. I was hoping to find that an ISDN line had been installed – the vital link that would connect us to Australia. Instead, surprise, surprise, two wires sticking out of the wall.

The phone chase began. I spoke to Mr Patel at All India Radio. Not to worry, he said, all we had to do was wait for the man from MTNL, Indian Telecom. We waited. No man. After innumerable conversations and three hours twiddling our thumbs, we decided to cut our losses and head back to the hotel, and hope that in fact all would be fixed as promised by the morning. We were even assured by the staff at All India Radio that the "man" had already arrived and was outside the ground working on our problem.

Next day, the morning of the match, we got to the ground at eight o'clock. The two wires were still there – and no man. What to do? Panic? Improvise. A little box had arrived and we set that up with our ISDN gear and stuck in a couple of cables and found a power plug. Channel Nine had very kindly linked us to their power rather than the local electricity, which is unreliable. As so often in the past they had also agreed to give us a feed of the effects from their microphones in the middle and a split of the television pictures. As I said, it helps to have mates. By a process of trial and error, and a little bit of nervousness, and no doubt some impatience back in Australia, Glenn and I were able to put the box of tricks together. The broadcast was up and running.

This wasn't the case throughout the match. There was, as always happens here, a breakdown because of a misunderstanding. It happened because we had two broadcast lines in – one for the ISDN unit, which is a very clean high quality signal, and the backup, an ordinary telephone line.

Now, the telephone line was what you might best describe, in old Australian terminology, like being on a party line in the country. Every time I made or received a call it seemed like Mrs Kafoops and the man next door were on the line. But it was only audible at my end. As I was hearing these dialogues, bursting in and garbling my own conversation, back in Australia they could only hear my voice. It was an annoyance and needed to be fixed. So a request was made to clear this cross-traffic from the line.

Unfortunately they took us up the wrong way and pulled the plug on the ISDN unit during the second day of the match. Kerfuffle ensued. For an hour and a half, live on national radio, we had to resort to using the mobile phone.

It was a bit like the old days of broadcasting

Say so... *"The All India Radio technician reached over and pulled the plug. We were immediately off the air. It was one of the few occasions when I lost it. It didn't come to blows ... but I do think I made the point."*

international matches, where you had the ball-by-ball man describing the whole over and then passing the phone to Peter Roebuck, Mike Coward or Greg Matthews to have their say. And all this against the constant background noise surging from the crowd, so unlike Australian fans who tend to be fairly quiet until something actually happens.

The reaction to this technical hitch varied. Our bosses at the ABC were less than impressed and threatened, I heard later, to take the broadcast off the air because a promise had been made to deliver a first-class signal from India. Had they done that, I can only imagine what reaction there would have been on the switchboard, because a number of people also called in to say that listening to the broadcast on the mobile phone gave them an authentic sense of actually being there. They loved it. This was reality, coming from another part of the world, and not just from another cricket ground that could have been anywhere.

Eventually the man arrived with a brand new phone and another little box, and after some further makeshift technical stuff was done, we were able to lock in and continue the broadcast.

As a postscript from the communication saga at the Wankhede Stadium, barely five minutes after the match concluded, I was on air and mid-sentence, almost mid-word with Mike Coward, when an energetic All India Radio technician raced in, reached over my shoulder and, totally unaware that a broadcast was taking place, pulled the plug. We were immediately off the air.

It was one of the few occasions when I lost it, for about five seconds. It didn't come to blows but I do think I made the point that he was unwelcome in the box and had no right to be pulling the plugs out.

That incident apart, we had a very good relationship with the All India team. They were very keen to help, and when they did turn up they came in numbers. I won't forget the sight of four men working on one plug to go into one socket in one wall – I guess it said much about the division of labour in this part of the world, where jobs are scarce and inefficiency at an all-time high.

As the somewhat shamefaced technician left the box, we all started to laugh. We managed to link up again and finish off the broadcast.

The game itself was a remarkable one. Australia won, and won decisively in the end, but there many periods during the Test match at Mumbai when it looked like the tourists were going to face a very powerful challenge.

This was mainly in the form of Sachin Tendulkar.

It's worth mentioning the adulation of the Indian fans towards the Australian players. This is mixed with a very passionate view of the game, and while the fans are keen on the star players they're not backward at coming forward with comments.

When Glenn Mitchell and I checked into our hotel, for instance, the staff member at the Oberoi, a chap called Arvind, told us he was a big fan of the Waugh brothers, but didn't hesitate to add that he felt India would win the series one-nil.

And when Adam Gilchrist arrived at the Taj Mahal, the team's hotel, he had an amusing encounter with the young man who was organising things around his room. The lad had an autograph book tucked under his arm and as he was doing various things for Gilchrist, he thrust it forward. The Australian vice-captain was quite happy, of course, to give him his autograph. As he handed the book back, the young man thanked him and said,

"I admire your batting very much. It is wonderful to see the way you play."

Adam Gilchrist made some polite response, but there was more to come.

"But I do think," the young man added, "you cut too early in your innings."

The drama really started against the bowling of Harbhajan Singh, the young off-spinner with the turban-like patka. From the commentary box we watched his little skipping approach, at this stage of the series still something of an unknown quantity.

To many people in India, the very name is almost a religion. He is a god. It was clear at the start of the Test match that most of the fans had come in the expectation of seeing him play.

And watching him in action again, it was clear that he is the best batsman in the world. The way he is able to pick the bowling off, his straight driving, his ability to judge the line and length and, with a flick of the wrists, dismiss the bowler down to fine leg or backward square, it was all extraordinary.

And the number of boundaries he hit sustained the tempo of his innings brilliantly.

Even before the match started there had been much speculation about what Australia would do with their team. They'd seen the pitch and I know Steve Waugh couldn't quite believe the amount of grass on it and thought it would be shaved a lot closer come the day of the match, but when they went out to toss, the pitch looked as green as the rest of the square.

For that reason Steve decided to go with three pace bowlers and Shane Warne, leaving out Colin Miller, a decision he must have dwelt on for some time, because according to the pundits the pitch would take some spin. How much was the big question mark. We were later to find out ... quite a bit.

He was mindful that India, short of some serious form and recent Test match cricket, might be a little underdone. His feeling was perhaps the same as it had been in Australia two seasons earlier when India succumbed to pace.

Clearly he thought that was Australia's best chance of getting on top of them – bowling, as he would describe it, to the game plan, keeping the ball on and outside the off stump. I could almost hear his voice, cool and dispassionate: "Keep it disciplined, keep it tight, dry them up and wait for the mistakes."

And that's pretty much how it panned out. They sent India in, we were treated to a marvellous innings of 76 from Tendulkar, and the rest of the batting fell away. They made only 176. McGrath was at his meanest best. He did not waver from that line of off stump and outside, bowling 19 overs and taking 3-19. Ominously, Shane Warne gained some enormous turn, an indication of the difficulty Australia might themselves face.

In reply Australia very quickly got themselves into bother. Within the first hour of the second day, Slater was clean bowled, his feet not quite working, getting an inside edge to a ball from Agarkar.

But the drama really started against the spin of Harbhajan Singh, a name we were to become familiar with as the series unfolded, but at this early stage still something of an unknown quantity.

A young man, only 23 years old, this off-spin bowler was easily identified in his patka, a turban-like piece of headwear with a bobble on the front. From the commentary box we studied his little skipping approach to the pitch, followed by his quite accurate, lobbing off-breaks. "He doesn't have a lot of variety but he's able to land them well enough," observed one of the experts, with considerable prescience.

It was the spinning ball that did it, spitting off the pitch from a length, trampolining around the throat of wicket-keeper Nayan Mongia and turning very sharply at times, and unpredictably. The ball was really taking a grip on the surface, which seemed shaky underneath, and so dry it was distintegrating to a powdery dust. Not every ball was doing this, but enough to cause concern. I had inspected the pitch at the start of the match, and Glenn had gone out subsequently to report on changes. He said he'd never seen a pitch like it.

In the bowlers' footmark areas and around where the batsmen stood it was like sand, or more correctly, silt. It was like fine, clay-coloured silt that was almost powdery.

Within an hour of the start Australia were struggling at 5-99. Then Adam Gilchrist, partnered by

Matthew Hayden playing as sensibly as I've ever seen him, started to mount a counterattack against the turning ball. It was just thrilling to watch.

Gilchrist is such a clean hitter – I think the cleanest I've seen since the days of Ian Botham. Botham may have been a more brutal player, but Gilchrist loses nothing by comparison, because of his ability to put the ball away, to judge the length, to go after the bowling and absolutely pummel it. He did have a stroke of luck on 44 when Bedani, the 12th man for India, missed a skier when running back on the leg side and in fact didn't even get a hand to it. But the onslaught continued unabated: Gilchrist hit 15 fours and four sixes in his innings, and got to his century before Hayden, who had given him quite a start. Their partnership really destroyed the confidence of the Indian bowlers. Gilchrist's hundred came off 84 balls, the second fastest by an Australian in Test history, surpassed only by Jack Gregory's 67-ball century almost 80 years ago, against South Africa in 1921-22.

India had to take some of the blame for all of this, and captain Sourav Ganguly's tactics were called into question when he took Venkatapathy Raju out of the attack as soon as he'd dismissed Steve Waugh, and plumped for Sachin Tendulkar's right-arm spin variations. Tendulkar was not accurate enough to consistently worry the batsmen.

There was additional disappointment for India

Say so... *"It's a matter of attitude and enjoying the culture and the surroundings. We're going to give it our best shot. If we get beaten, India are going to have to play real good cricket."* **Steve Waugh**

when speedster Javagal Srinath bowled a couple of very poor overs at the start of the day and then left the field, having sustained a whack on his right index finger when he was batting. He wasn't seen again until much later in proceedings, when he did manage to get Hayden out, caught behind. By then the damage had been done. Shane Warne joined in the excitement,

clouting three sixes. The score had
gone to 349.

That evening I ran into David
Hookes in the bar and sat down for a
quiet drink which became a longer
session than I'd intended.

He has become the Australian
voice of Foxtel coverage, working with
TWI mainly, and has made a niche for
himself as a television commentator.

He's also a broadcaster on 3AW in
Melbourne, doing a sport talkback show, and he likes
calling the Australian Rules too.

David is a man with an opinion on a number of
things in life, not only on cricket and Australian Rules
football, and he enjoys having a wager on it. Like a lot
of us who are close to the action he believes that we
should back our opinion with our cash.

It's a very Australian thing. We often swap notes on
tour – just talking about bets and about the game.

He's very close to cricket obviously, because he was
a fine player. If you look at Charles Davis's statistics in
the 2001 Ashes Tour edition of the "ABC Cricket
Book" on the fastest scoring batsmen (ie runs per 100
balls faced), he's right up there in Anglo-Australian
matches. In 11 Ashes Test matches he scored at 59 per
100 balls, and was seventh fastest of all time, one place
ahead of Bradman. (See box, above)

He had an intermittent international career.
including the decisive years of World Series Cricket. He
was a bit of a one-dimensional player, an Adelaide Oval
specialist who'd stand and deliver. Against spin bowling
his technique was too loose, but he was a great hand-
eye player. He didn't quite have the game to succeed
consistently at Test level – but he was a dashing,
exciting player and a plunderer in Shield cricket.

His debut in Test cricket was a famous one – he
hit five boundaries in an over from Tony Greig at
the MCG in the 1977 Centenary Test.

With that introduction to international cricket, he
had to live with the tag of a potential superstar

The 10 fastest scoring batsmen* in Ashes history are as follows:			
Team	Batsman	Runs per 100 balls	Tests
England	APF Chapman	65	16
England	IT Botham	63	36
Australia	SJ McCabe	62	24
Australia	VT Trumper	61	40
Australia	J Darling	60	31
Australia	JM Gregory	60	21
Australia	DW Hookes	59	11
Australia	DG Bradman	59	37
Australia	IA Healy	56	33
England	FE Woolley	56	32

thereafter. In the series in '82-3 against England in Australia, he didn't make 100 but he scored a lot of half-centuries. And he hit the ball superbly. He was really on in that series.

Perhaps he was one of those cricketers with whom it's just a question of time and place.

While David and I were talking that evening in Mumbai, Colin Miller, who'd probably been a little unlucky to be left out of the team, came down and joined us at the bar. We discussed the condition of the pitch – he thought that with such a good lead Australia could win the game very decisively. All of a sudden the ball was misbehaving. He talked interestingly about his development as a spin bowler and how much he'd learnt in the couple of years since he'd made his debut against Pakistan in Rawalpindi in 1998.

He'd come into the top-level game very late in his cricketing life, and he'd got to the point where he now had more variety, more ammunition, and more options.

As the match went on, it was clear that Miller's bowling was missed by the Australian side. In the wash-up, if you were naming your best eleven for that pitch, he should have played. But as it turned out, it didn't really matter.

On air next day, Peter Roebuck and I talked about the spin bowling during the commentary, assessing particularly how the spinners must operate to be successful in India.

Peter, as always, came up with a good line. He recalled the wise words of advice once delivered by India's famous spinner Erapally Prasanna, who along with Bishen Bedi and Bhagwat Chandrasekhar, had done such a magnificent job for the Indian team back in the 1960s and '70s.

Prasanna's mantra to spin bowlers was simple: "Length is mandatory, line is optional." And that is probably where, under the assault from Gilchrist, the Indian spin bowlers had wavered.

Once again, the stumbling block in the second innings was Sachin Tendulkar. There was some early resistance from Ramesh till he showed very poor

Hookes, Henry and "the sting"

....

A MEMORABLE, COMICAL DAY OF INFAMY AT THE SCG

I still remember the famous day at the SCG when NSW played South Australia and, with the objective of keeping the game alive, there was allegedly some collusion between "Henry" Lawson, the NSW captain, and David Hookes, the South Australian captain, about NSW declaring at a certain point. In order to do that South Australia had to bowl spinners and keep the field up, which they did. But then it got to a point where NSW obviously decided that things were going quite well, so they'd let it ride. Hookes, having been led to expect they would close, was furious.

Steve Waugh referred to it later in the day, I think, as "the sting", and Lawson certainly got Hookes classically. They kept batting on, Hookes took umbrage of course, and had bowlers deliberately bowl wides. There was all sorts of swearing going on out in the field about NSW tactics, and it really did get pretty base.

> THERE WAS A "GENTLEMAN'S" AGREEMENT TO KEEP THE GAME ALIVE. UNFORTUNATELY, THEY WEREN'T ALL GENTLEMEN.

The next day I did a lengthy interview with Hookes, questioning him on the way he had behaved, pointing out that quite a few people had called the ABC, enraged about the language in the field. They'd had children there, they said, where was the value system, what was the game coming to … that sort of thing.

David very articulately defended his tactical position, if not the team's behaviour. I thought then that he might have a future as a cricket commentator, as an analyser of events. That's exactly what he does on television — it's a difficult role in that you've got to be cryptic, you've got to get it right, and it's hard to come up with the precise words for the moment.

He's doing a good job at Foxtel, but since he's not in the Channel Nine fold, he tends only to get the exposure in Australia when we are playing away from home.

The Australians were always thinking that there was going to be a way to conjure a wicket, even when a good partnership was going. It was not just a measure of their confidence but of their self-belief.

composure, waving at one outside the off stump, and McGrath claimed another wicket.

However, when Tendulkar was at the crease, and while he was there with Rahul Dravid and batting throughout the pre-lunch session on the third day, there seemed some hope that India might be able to reel in the deficit, get on equal terms and then create a target for Australia in the final innings.

Watching Tendulkar play with such measured confidence and control, I wondered how the Australians would make a breakthrough. But it probably sums up the self-belief of the Australian side to say that they bowled with expectation. They were always thinking that there was going to be a way to conjure a wicket, even when a good partnership was going. It was not just a measure of their confidence but of their belief that this would occur.

How it happened is worth recounting in detail. It was freakish, and exactly the kind of turn of events that changes matches and marks the difference between teams that take their opportunities and the rest.

Justin Langer had quite a deal to do with this. He had saved a number of runs at short leg by standing his ground unflinchingly when the ball was hit in his direction. There may have been occasions when it was purely accidental and he just couldn't get out of the way, but he was a serious road block to a number of these strokes.

Damien Fleming had been unable to do much with his variety of fast off-spin, and Steve Waugh threw the ball to brother Mark to see if his version of off-spin would have any more luck. This was what tempted Tendulkar to play a pull shot.

Langer, sensing what was about to happen, half-turned away and the ball smashed into him just under his left shoulder blade. It looped up into the air towards mid-wicket, where Ricky Ponting took off, diving full length, and clutched a miraculous catch.

Tendulkar was out for 65. With that break the Indian innings just fell apart.

Shane Warne, who had shown his respect for

Tendulkar by bowling around the wicket, resumed against Dravid. He had batted for over four hours for 39, and he was bowled by a huge leg break, pitching, turning and actually hitting the off stump. Signs of Warne regaining his powers and breadth of spin!

The innings ended on a bizarre note, with Srinath coming out to bat one-handed. It was as if he was out there under protest, perhaps under instruction from Ganguly. At the crease, he held the bat with his top hand, moved to one side and waved at the ball. It was an embarrassment that luckily didn't last too long – McGrath pitched one on line, Srinath missed it and that was the end of the innings at 219 all out.

The Australians required very few to win and they polished them off in seven overs. Hayden and Slater secured that 16th consecutive win.

The match was over with an hour to spare on the third day. As I read through the scorecard on air during the wrap-up of our coverage, there was a memorable scene on the field. The Australians did a relaxed and casual lap of honour, and many of the Indian fans stayed. I watched Matthew Hayden and a number of others going along the fence, topped by barbed wire, with hundreds of hands reaching through, touching them all as they went by.

As they had done earlier in the tour at a press conference, the players gained enormous credibility. It was a warm and usefully diplomatic gesture.

One incident in the First Test caused a degree of unpleasantness and attracted adverse comment that was to go on long after the match was over.

At the centre of it was Michael Slater, whose

predisposition to "brain explosions" I've noted earlier. Not strictly relevant to this controversy, but an interesting sidelight on it, was the fact that late on the first day Slater had been given not out caught behind. To us in the box it looked like a clear edge through to the keeper but English umpire David Shepherd shook his head. He must have had second thoughts, however, because on leaving the field at the close of play he said to David Hookes, "Did you burn me?" Hookes had no doubts – the television replay showed the ball clearly hitting the outside edge.

Shep was straightforward about it.

"I didn't hear anything," he said, "although I thought from Slater's body language that he might have hit it. There just wasn't a sound to prove quite clearly to me that he'd snicked the ball."

Shepherd's decision had little effect on the flow of the game, as Slater was out early next day. But it was interesting later in the game in relation to the event which generated so much controversy.

Rahul Dravid was going along nicely in the Indian second innings and had reached 22 when he went for a pull shot from Fleming's bowling. The ball may have stopped on him a little bit, he miscued in the direction of square leg and Slater, coming in after initially going back, lunged forward and grabbed the ball. He held it

Say so... "*The umpires in the field were uncertain, perhaps unsighted, and referred it to the third umpire. The replay was at best inconclusive. There was doubt all round, and no option but to give the green light.*"

up, offering the ball towards the batsman and clearly indicating that he had made the catch. Dravid, naturally, looked to the umpire. David Shepherd, perhaps unsighted at square leg, and umpire Venkat were uncertain and referred it to the third umpire. Nerendra Menon duly studied the replay, which was at best inconclusive. There was doubt all round, so he had no option but to give the green light.

The evidence, I thought, was quite strong that the

Steve Waugh holds a replica of the famous urn after his team retained the Ashes.

Tendulkar blurs out his contemporaries.

Colin Miller drops Lara at the SCG; he quickly made amends.

McGrath celebrates his Test hat-trick in Perth.

Matthew Hayden and Michael Slater after scoring the winning runs in Mumbai.

Warne bowls Atherton around his legs at Lord's.

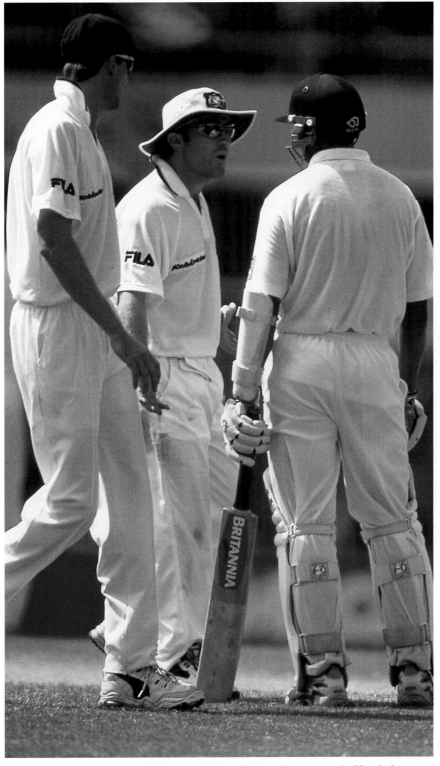

Michael Slater and Rahul Dravid struggle for a diplomatic outcome in Mumbai.

The surest hands in international cricket: Mark Waugh's perfect technique.

ball had touched the ground as Slater took it. Slater, however, was beside himself. He's a man given to his emotions and he overreacted. Initially he appeared to remonstrate with umpire Venkat, then as if it was a matter of honour, he went up to Dravid and appeared to challenge him. We couldn't hear his words but they appeared to be along the lines of – "Look, I've caught the ball, don't you accept me at my word? Are you questioning my integrity?"

Dravid just stood there. He was clearly uncertain at the time of the catch and like all the players had waited for the umpire's decision. He was given not out and that was that. As Slater walked away he seemed to say something unpleasant in Dravid's direction.

I think this was something that Slater was reminded of at lunchtime when the match referee, Cammie Smith, met with him, Australian coach John Buchanan and manager Steve Bernard. Cammie Smith is one of the more friendly of the match referees on the circuit and I think it's his desire to stay friendly that makes him a soft option arbiter.

Slater got away with a reprimand, and in this case was obviously fortunate not to receive worse.

It brought back memories of an incident that Slater was involved in, though as the "wronged" party, with Venkatesh Prasad in the 1999-2000 series in Australia. Pace bowler Prasad had given Slater a send-off when he had him caught on the hook shot, and for his pains was fined by the match referee on that occasion. This new offence on Slater's part appeared to be far more serious, and for the sake of consistency if nothing else, deserved more than a slap on the wrist.

At the end of the match Steve Waugh was straight up about it. He said he thought Slater had overreacted and that the players were very conscious of the need not to do so. This was a wake-up call to them, a reminder that this was not the way to behave.

The pity of it was that Waugh didn't move more quickly to prevent what occurred on the field. Two seconds of reaction from him would have been enough – even if he agreed in some way with what Slater had

Slater was beside himself. We couldn't hear his words to the batsman, Rahul Dravid, but they were clearly along the lines of – "I've caught the ball, don't you accept me at my word? Are you questioning my integrity?" Dravid just stood there.

been aggrieved about – there would have been an easy way to defuse the situation on the spot.

It brought home the importance of the strength of the captain on the field. It's even written in the laws of cricket that it's the duty of the captain to uphold the spirit of the game.

And perhaps Steve took note of that himself at the time. It would be nice to know that if it ever happened again he would jump in and immediately pour water on the flames.

In a country like India, particularly where there are volatile crowds, this is far from academic. One could only imagine what would happen if it were Tendulkar and not Dravid at the centre of it or, say, at Calcutta or Chennai in a very tight situation in the game.

I know it's a long time since it occurred on an Australian tour, nevertheless it does happen. Back in 1969-70 Venkataraghavan, now the umpire, was given out and the radio commentators at the time suggested that he hadn't hit the ball. This caused a tremendously volatile reaction from the crowd and there was a riot during that match.

It could happen again. Perhaps it was a good lesson for Slater to have learnt. For his captain too.

The Test match had finished, but that night our hotel was the setting for a cricket event of a different kind. A display of Australian cricket memorabilia, which included a lot of signed Bradman photographs from a private collection, were going to be auctioned. It was the first time that an auction of this type had been put on in India, and it would test the water. Similar auctions around the world have fetched significant amounts.

Glenn Mitchell and I ate an early dinner in the hotel's Frangipani Restaurant, then headed up to the pool deck area to check out the auction.

Former Australian captain Kim Hughes was one of the entrepreneurs involved. I'd run into him on a couple of occasions at the match and he'd admitted he was nervous about the outcome. Of course it had been planned a while ago, and it was no fault of the people putting it on that Bradman had died two days before. It was either a fortunate or an unfortunate coincidence, depending on which perspective you took on it.

For an auction it was quite an extraordinary event. It was a lavish affair, with no expense spared – a glossy catalogue, video screens of Bradman in action, and tables on the lawn groaning with free food and drink to cater to the cream of Bombay society, including all the stars of the huge Mumbai "Bollywood" movie industry. The local television stations turned up, with arc lighting everywhere, and as auctioneer there was Tom Alter, a smooth-talking local filmstar, famous I was told for his roles as the villain in many Hindi movies. He had the job, the difficult job as it turned out, of trying to elicit money from the people who had turned up.

There's no pleasant way of saying this – given the build-up, the outcome was just a horrible flop. The Bradman name may be revered in India, but that's not the same thing as getting people to part with money for a piece of memorabilia, a picture or an autograph.

As you walked in you were issued with a paddle with a number that you were supposed to thrust into the air as you made a bid. It was fairly clear from the start, when the first item of Bradmania was put up for auction at $US750 opening bid, that it was going to be a tough night. There were no paddles in the air, no bids. Eventually when this price was reduced after negotiation to $US500, it did attract one bidder – I think perhaps one of the related parties.

Around six or eight of the first items were passed in. Then there was a change in the batting order, perhaps in an attempt to excite a little more interest. All of a sudden we saw wicket-keeping gloves with the signatures "Warne" and "Healy" on them and these eventually did in fact sell for $US1600. The contemporary stuff seemed to be more valued than Sir Donald's. I think the highest price was fetched by a stump from the tied Test in Madras, which went for $US2000, though according to Kim Hughes something of this order had already been paid for it in Australia.

The final poke in the eye for the entrepreneurs was when the Bollywood actor was seen desperately looking for bids for a cricket bat signed by both the Australian and Indian teams, the proceeds of which were going to go to the earthquake victims in Gujurat. He started as usual with a ridiculously high initial price – he kicked the bidding off at $US2500 – and after one or two embarrassing minutes of trying to draw just one bid, he offered to put up $US1000 of his own money if

Kim Hughes, the casualty

A GIFTED, WONDERFUL PLAYER, AUSTRALIA'S GOLDEN CAPTAIN OF THE EARLY 1980S HAD A FATAL FLAW.

As a cricketer, Kim Hughes was a casualty of himself. He was a very gifted, wonderful player and in a different era under different management may have been more successful. The captaincy wore him down, there's no doubt about it. He was playing in a side that wasn't 100 per cent behind him, and was erratic in his own leadership too. He played some magnificent innings for Australia, but in the way he led his life, I suppose you could say he was prone to errors of judgment. Perhaps with better influences around him he would have grown through that period.

He came into the Australian team as an outstanding talent, but he averaged 37.42 in Test cricket, which for a player of his ability isn't a class career set of numbers.

When he was batting, it was if there was a trigger in his brain. He'd decide in advance he was going to hit a ball for four, and couldn't discipline himself to play the bowling as he saw it. He had to impose himself in some way. He had what you might call these rushes of blood shots.

I can remember in the West Indies, when he was captain of the side and under enormous pressure because they were losing, he hit a delivery from a slow bowler down the ground for four. The West Indies dropped a fieldsman out to long on ... and what did Hughes do? ... he hit it straight someone else would kick in with the other $US1500. Not even that was able to draw a bid from the crowd, many of whom were still busily stuffing themselves with the free food and drinks.

By the end of the auction, we reckoned that of the 70-odd items in the catalogue, only 20 had been purchased, mainly for close to their reserve mark, over 20 had been passed in and more than 30 had not even been offered. By our collation something like $US22,000 had been raised from the auction. Now, I would have thought that wouldn't have covered anything near the costs of putting it on.

It would have brought little comfort to the organisers some months later to note the comments of a Christie's auctioneer on Bradman's 1948 baggy green.

"I know where it is. I know who owns it. Since Bradman's death it has increased in value – $250,000 is probably being too conservative."

down his throat. Just an act of insanity.

In his final Test match before his lacrimose departure from the Australian side, Hughes said that he wasn't going to hook. Now, for a guy who attacked the bowling as he did, he was really backing himself into a corner. So, of course, the first bouncer that came along he did hook and holed out to long leg. He put unnecessary pressure on himself.

Admittedly, he suffered from the fact that he was leading the side after the divisive experience of World Series Cricket. There was clearly a bit of an "us and them" attitude, and Lillee and Marsh particularly didn't seem to respect him as a leader. Maybe the decision-makers at the time would have been better off burying the hatchet and giving Rodney Marsh the captaincy — at least there would have been some sort of solidity. Maybe

Marsh would have been a better captain.

Also, Hughes didn't have the captaincy in his own right after World Series, because Greg Chappell came back to lead the team at home and then announced that he didn't want to tour in '81. Hughes took the team to England, and as we now know, for Australia it was a disaster, with Botham turning the Headingley Test around, inspiring an English victory.

Ultimately, Hughes resigned as captain in 1984 and went and played in South Africa on the rebel tours. As a result of that he was banned for life by the WA Cricket Association, later overturned.

It was a combination of factors that worked against Kim, but most of all he couldn't keep a level head about him to focus on what was important. In any other era, he might have been an outstanding success for a longer time.

Time Out

EARLY FINISHES IN TEST MATCHES ARE
DISAPPOINTING TO FANS AND PLAYERS, BUT
FOR AUSTRALIA THREE-DAYERS HAVE BECOME A
FACT OF LIFE. AT LEAST FOR THOSE OF US
FOLLOWING THE TOUR, THERE WAS THE BONUS
OF TIME OFF IN A LAND OF SURPRISES.

For the players, broadcasters and journalists alike, one of the pluses of a three-day finish in a Test match is the opportunity to see the sights. Neither Glenn Mitchell nor I needed persuading.

The morning after the premature end to the First test, on a day blanketed with Mumbai's ever-present smog, we walked from the hotel along what they call the Queen's Necklace, the ribbon of lights of Marine Parade that is part of the point that defines Mumbai.

Originally when the Portuguese settled here in the 16th century it would have been all swamp – the land was reclaimed and it's on a foundation of seven islands that modern Mumbai, a city of 15 million inhabitants, is built.

There's a good sea wall there and it's needed – although it's some seven or eight metres high, in typhoon conditions the water does in fact climb the wall and bounce across the thoroughfare.

After half an hour's walk along Marine Parade you come to Mumbai's famous Chowpatty Beach. And though it's said that the locals do swim there, I think it's safe to say that Bondi's reputation is still intact.

It's a fascinating part of town, however, where even modest-looking apartments change hands for well over $US1 million. Harsha Bhogle lives near here.

It's most famous for its many street performers, though when we were there we didn't see anyone lying on a bed of nails or eating fire – fakirs or fakers, you can decide for yourself.

We were taken aback by an amazing wreck of a motor car that had been pushed off the road on to the beach. It had once been a very proud black Mercedes-Benz ... and it was pulverised.

It looked as though it had rolled over 20 times, all the panels were knocked in, there wasn't a single centimetre of it that wasn't mangled. We asked a policeman what had occurred and he said it had lost control one night and all three occupants had been killed. Glenn's imagination was fired by this, with a scenario of underworld heists and car chases that would have put Bollywood to shame.

Some of the team in the ABC commentary box.
Pictured clockwise from the author, Jim Maxwell, in cap; journalist Mike Coward; Harsha Bhogle; Mr Subramanian; and Greg Matthews beside a visiting English friend on his right.

From there we took a cab and went to the Crawford Markets, street after street of shops and stalls, where there's constant hustle and bustle and you get the chance to lay your hands on just about anything you might need. In my case this meant a small screwdriver I needed to help me out with running repairs on the radio equipment.

We finished up in a little bar having a Fanta and a Limca, a little lime juice. The waiter presented the change on a bed of aniseed, which is used, I guess, to help cleanse your palate.

The markets themselves were amazing – you could close your eyes for a moment amid the throng of people, forget the sight of anything motorised and you were transported to a long-gone age. There were fellows dragging carts around, others carrying empty oil cans or mysterious packages on their heads, someone else on a bicycle draped with about 100 bags of produce – it was a shantyville of shopkeepers, artisans and humanity of every description.

In addition to my newly acquired screwdriver, I was looking for a bag to carry some of our mechanical

Say so... *"The stallholder and I couldn't agree on a price and so I walked out, thinking I'd be called back. But no, he'd made his mind up and my last bid was 10 rupees short. The things you'll do to save 40 cents."*

equipment, and the quest turned into an instructive exercise in bartering. Eventually the stallholder and I couldn't agree on a price and so I walked out, thinking that I'd be called back in time-honoured fashion. That's how the bazaar works, right? But no, he'd made his mind up and wasn't going to go any lower than 110 rupees for this bag.

My last bid was 100, so we were on our way, and the bag was never purchased. The things you'll do to save 40 cents!

That evening we decided to take in one of the local restaurants. We were recommended a place called the

Khyber, about five minutes by taxi from the hotel. It looked like Aladdin's Cave, with nooks and crannies everywhere, and the food was magnificent, particularly the lamb dish we started with, beautifully spiced and served off the bone.

Leaving the Khyber, we went nosing around – there's always a startling scene that confronts you in a city like Mumbai – and there, just 200 metres along the road, was a family sleeping on the street.

There must have been six or seven babies, with all the family's possessions spread around, and a fire going, with some sort of basic bubble and squeak cooking away. Their clothes were little more than rags and one of the men was trying to smash up some foraged wood to keep the fire alight.

They didn't need it for warmth, just for cooking, but it made me wonder how on earth these people could survive in the monsoon. Where would they shelter when the rains came?

This became a familiar sight in various places around Mumbai, but even so I must say the cleanliness of the streets was impressive. People went out of their way to keep the place spotless. Even where they slept beside the road, they would use little brushes to make things as clean as possible before spreading out a shawl or some other material to lie on.

It's a cliche, I suppose, but India is a land of contrasts. Among the most amazing sights in Mumbai were the large roundabouts at the many intersections. These were truly magnificent gardens, full of orchids and all sorts of tropical vegetation.

On one particular middle-of-the-road garden was a proud notice that it had won first prize in a competition. On one hand, in the slum areas you could see all sorts of detritus and unpleasantness and absolute squalor, elsewhere the place was spotlessly clean. The locals had a high regard for keeping it that way too.

The following day, in the care of our taxi-driver Nana, we headed out to what is called the Dhobi Ghat, an immense open-air laundry. It is a vast, and sacred

The last thing most people think if they've never been to India is to venture out and eat anywhere but in a hotel. In fact, if you've got a reasonably steady stomach that can handle spicier food, you're not at any more risk than eating in the hotel. It seemed absurd that in the hotel where we were staying, there was a great variety of dishes but only two of them local. They were so keen, it seemed, to look after the eating habits of the Westerner there were more pizzas and burgers than their own food. It surprised me, particularly when we saw so many locals eating there too, but then maybe the Frangipani Restaurant at the Oberoi was a place to be seen.

Don't Dally in Delhi

SUNIL GAVASKAR TAUGHT US A LESSON IN FATALISM

You need cool nerves when you're being driven in Delhi, and most other places in India. Near-misses are frequent, and sometimes you don't miss at all. Although there are actual lane markings on the road, particularly in Delhi, where you may have

four or five lanes operating at once, with the combination of motor scooters, tuk-tuks, auto-rickshaws, taxis and trucks, all concertinaed and all fighting desperately to get to the front of the queue at the traffic lights, it's first in best dressed. Sudden turns to right or left are normal.

I think the best example of it all is at roundabouts. Normally (ie in Australia) anyone entering a roundabout gives way to those who are already on it. In India, if you're coming into a roundabout, look out … if you're already on it … look out, because every other driver will just take off and grab the first possible position. It's a bit like Indian life in general. There is no such thing as queuing, you just go for broke. And when space is so limited, it's understandable that you'd want to be at the head of a queue, as it were — if there was one.

I always think of Sunil Gavaskar, the former Indian captain, when I think of Indian traffic. Travelling with us in a car, he would sit in the front seat and turn and face the passengers in the back for a discussion. After a while, going back and forth every day between the hotel and the ground, I asked him why he never looked

at the road ahead.

"Well it's a sense of fatalism," he said. "If there's going to be an accident, I don't want to see it."

That's India.
Live for the moment, not for tomorrow.

Say so... *"I joined in a game of kids' cricket in the back streets of Delhi, and I have to say it brought a fleeting memory of my own early days of street cricket. Same idea, same game, but what a different world."*

place, with row after row of washing troughs and little cubicles, where people constantly rinse and thrash their clothes against stone walls to get the water out, then with an enormous soaping down start the process all over again. There must have been hundreds of people whacking away with the clothes, and behind them were great rows of sheets and clothes all strung out.

On the periphery of all this a game of kids' cricket was going on. I went down and joined in and bowled a couple of balls with these street children. They were using a tennis ball that had had all its hair shaved off, but it was quite firm, so they must have put something inside to give it the feel of a fairly solid squash ball and a much firmer bounce.

It was cricket in an alley, their way of amusing themselves, and I have to say it brought a fleeting memory of my own early days of street cricket. Same idea, same game, but what a different world.

Afterwards we wove around to Falkland Road where they have what is called the Cages, the bordello area of Mumbai. Not a very pleasant sight at all, here were women sitting or standing around outside small cubicle-like rooms, in which we could see straight through to where there was a bed behind a curtain. Given that India has produced so many Miss Worlds, it was clear that none of them came from or went back to this particular part of town.

We stopped in a nearby street to take some pictures of a little child with a plastic cricket bat. Outside the run-down house, his family had set up an old-fashioned Singer sewing machine and were at work on some fabric making some sort of clothing.

It made for a lovely photo, with this kid beaming a smile and the whole of the family gathering around him, although the Muslim women were a little

Say so... *"We saw the Towers of Silence, where the Parsees lay out their dead to be picked off by the vultures. You can't actually see the bodies, the Towers are well shielded by trees, which I have to say is a good thing."*

embarrassed about being seen and quickly had a veil up to cover their faces.

In the afternoon we had arranged with another drive, Shubash, to take us to see the famous Hanging Garden, which isn't exactly hanging but is certainly at a high point, Malabar Hill, with sweeping views down over Back Bay and Chowpatty Beach.

Behind are the Towers of Silence, where the Parsees lay out their dead to be picked off by the vultures. A religious sect with origins in Persia, the Parsees hold fire, earth and water sacred, and therefore choose not to cremate or bury their dead.

You can't actually see the bodies, the Towers are well shielded by trees, which I have to say is a good thing. A few years ago a major international publisher, Time-Life, disregarded the sanctity of the Parsees' practices and shot photographs from overhead, which were subsequently published in a book. This intrusion didn't go down well and the magazine was banned by all the distributors in India as a result.

In the Hanging Garden itself, the most extraordinary thing is the hedges, which are beautifully cut in the shapes of the cow and the calf and the tiger – top topiary in fact. There was even a continuous hedge of mint, quite unlike anything I'd ever seen before.

The Second Test was scheduled to begin in Calcutta in a week's time on March 11, and in the interim Australia were to play a three-day game with the Board President's XI at Delhi. We farewelled Mumbai early in the morning to catch the two hour flight to Delhi. Here Glenn and I parted ways for a little while; he went down to Agra to see the Taj Mahal and, having been to Agra on a previous trip, I stuck around in Delhi. It was probably just as well because the news came through that Adam Gilchrist had a slight hip injury and Brad Haddin was going to be sent from Australia, which meant that all of a sudden on the day we arrived there was a quick press conference that I needed to attend.

Errol Alcott, the team physio, gave us some analysis of the injury to Gilchrist, only a minor one.

The vice-captain/wicket-keeper himself played down the injury as something that wouldn't trouble him for more than a moment or two, but he'd take the opportunity for a rest anyway. There was no doubt about him being ready for the Test match.

Signs of the Times

We had to smile, by the way, at the signage everywhere, all with a particularly Indian flavour. How about a no parking sign that cautions: "Parking Strictly Prohibited. Tyres will be deflated." Or the internet ad spruiking "Take your girlfriend places where her ex-boyfriend never did".

And then there were the pictorial signs in one park, little figures with a diagonal red bar across them, whose message was graphically clear: no littering ... no spitting ... no peeing in public. Activities that could be seen at any given moment in most places you might choose to look!

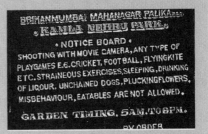

In the coming and going of taxi rides from the Oberoi Delhi, where I was staying, to the team's headquarters at the Taj Mahal, of course I ended up at the wrong hotel – which so often happens.

It was my bad instructions, I think, though on other occasions the taxi drivers are at fault.

And sure enough, it happened again that very evening. I'd been invited to attend a reception for the team at the Australian High Commission, and in attempting to get there from the hotel inevitably found myself outside the Austrian Embassy. Confusion and redirection ensued.

When I finally got to the right place I caught up with Jonathan Harley, the ABC representative in Delhi, and his wife Sarah, along with Christopher Kremmer, who is based in Delhi and writes for *The Sydney Morning Herald*, and used to be a long-time ABC correspondent.

All the Australian players were there enjoying the

Aussie! Aussie! Aussie!

IN A PACKED INDIAN CRICKET STADIUM PULSATING
WITH EXCITEMENT, IT TAKES A BRAVE SOUL TO
STAND UP AND BARRACK FOR THE AUSSIES.

That's exactly what a small band of diehard supporters did during this series. In fact it's what they've been doing at cricket locations around the world for a number of years. This downunder version of England's Barmy Army is led by a man called Luke Gallion, also mysteriously known as Lukey Sparrow.

I ran into him after the Mumbai Test match and took the chance to get his views on cricket stadiums, Indian police chiefs, takeaway food Indian-style, toilet facilities and more...

JM: Luke, you and the boys were at the First Test in Mumbai. What has your reception been like from the Indian crowd?

LG: Typically Indian. It was welcoming to begin but the Indians have a personal vendetta when it comes to opposition support. We were certainly outnumbered, we expected that, but there was greater intimidation than I've felt in any cricket stadium around the world. They just don't let up.

They don't actually say anything. It's the throwing of food, the throwing of cups, plush surroundings of a massive outdoor garden party under the stars, with a barbecue of Australian beef, a rare culinary experience, given that beef is on the prohibited list in this mainly Hindu nation. We were entertained by a Melbourne band, The Hoodangers, who were based in Mumbai.

One of the guests was Bishen Bedi, the legendary left-arm spinner and former Indian captain, immaculate in his turban. Chatting to him, I found him charming as always and more than willing to share his strong views about the bereft condition that Indian cricket had fallen into in recent years. As he saw it, the rot had started with the success of the Indian side in the 1983 World

anything that's not held down. Very parochial, of course, but they don't have a great deal of confidence in whoever is playing at any particular time.

They may call "Sachin, Sachin, Sachin" ... but if he doesn't perform they start calling "Agarkar, Agarkar, Agarkar" ... if he doesn't perform, maybe they'll go back to Sachin. It just doesn't let up through the whole day.

They live for now and they live for the ball. They're passionate about cricket but all they want is the next ball to go over the fence or the next three batsmen to go out so Sachin can come in.

JM: I did hear some sort of chant about the Aussies at the First Test.

LG: There are a lot of misconstrued sayings on the Indian terraces. More often than not it was "Australia sucks" or "Slater sucks" or "Mark Waugh sucks" ... they just went through the whole team.

JM: What about the food?

LG: You're best bringing your own food and drink, however the rules say that you're not allowed to. So the idea is to try to bring a little bit of contra tucked away in a few hidden pockets. Australians were given some leniency and we were allowed to bring in some water bottles. The food and beverages available are very limited and focused on the Indian diet of course, so everything is fried.

Then the police swept through and cleared all the vendors out and there was nothing to buy, not even an ice-cream.

We saw toilet facilities being built in the week before the Test commenced and we thought, this will be interesting. They were palatial ... marble tiles wall to wall, on the floor, even the ceiling. I thought, gee, this is quite fashionable.

But when I actually stood there, I wondered what was this splashing on the floor ... and looked down. It was just a hole at the bottom of the urinal going into a trough, blocked of course. Image is everything in India. It looked good, but they always seem to reach a point where

LG: Very low budget. That has been the reason I've been able to go around for so long, you know, rather than just throw money away in hotels with the amenities, such as air-conditioning and TVs. It's just not required. Where we're staying here, it's OK, there's four of us in one room, we're paying $4 each. And we've still got the colour TV.

JM: When the Australians did their lap of honour I got the impression that the

"THEY JEERED US ALL DAY, YET AS SOON AS AUSTRALIA WON THEY WERE THE FIRST TO OFFER THEIR HANDSHAKES."

they say, "Well, that's enough plumbing." Still, you've got to get a good laugh.

JM: You all had flags to wave. You must have developed a very good relationship with the police because normally they don't allow anyone to take anything into the ground.

LG: We've learnt the day before the game to find the chief of police or second-in-command and explain the situation. The person we spoke with at Mumbai was very understanding when I said there's going to be 30 of us in the crowd. We're not going to throw our cameras, we're not going to use anything as a missile or a flagpole as weapon.

He said, "Yeah, that's fine, any problems come and see me." When we turned up on Day One we were told we couldn't bring anything in, and so it was a case of demanding to see our contact.

When we spoke to him, he got on the phone and said, "There's 30 Australian supporters out there, let 'em in."

JM: And what sort of living conditions do you guys have on tour?

Indian fans were genuinely appreciative of what the team had done. How did you read it from your side of the fence?

LG: I actually find the Indians to be very sportsmanlike. Back at the '96 World Cup, they jeered us all day, yet at the end, as soon as Australia won, they were the first to congratulate us. The prime culprits, you know, for the missiles and everything, were the first to offer their handshakes.

JM: Is the solidarity of your group going to continue for as long as Australia wins — or as soon as the unbeaten record ends, will that see the group break up?

LG: I don't believe so. The people I've met on this particular tour want to go to England, they want to go to South Africa in a year's time, and the World Cup in the West Indies after that. And I think win or lose, people are going to go. The experience of following cricket around the world is so unique. Just to soak up the idea that you are in another continent watching your team play ... it's everything you need to send you to the next destination.

Cup, a shock victory that had concentrated Indian attention enormously on one-day cricket, with an overwhelming emphasis on the electronic media and the sponsors to embrace it. Certainly money had come to the board and to the players as a result, but the net effect was the loss of a generation of spin bowlers.

Unlike the days when Prasanna, Bedi and Chandrasekhar had so dominated batsmen around the world, now India found itself in the first decade of the new millennium with Anil Kumble as its one quality spin bowler. It was a parlous state of affairs, with no new spinners on the horizon and Kumble out of action this series with a shoulder injury.

To Bishen Bedi, the Indian board had seen the financial gain they could get from one-day cricket and had failed to develop players for the five-day game, and he really rued the fact. I did not discuss Harbhajan Singh's First Test performance in any detail. With the benefit of hindsight, I rather wish I had.

In the lead-up to the three-day game against the Board President's XI at the unprepossessing Feroz Shah Kotla ground in Delhi, Michael Kasprowicz jokingly said to the Indian media that he was looking forward to getting an opportunity to play. Because of the Australian "rotation" policy of player selection, he had missed the previous match in Mumbai.

"In any case," he added, "my batting is more impressive than my bowling so far."

The Feroz Shah Kotla Stadium is the most undistinguished international ground I've ever visited. Inevitably the taxi driver struggled to find it, and it took about six sets of directions from different people before we finally rolled up to be met by a massive security presence. It seemed there would be more policemen than spectators at the ground, though a few thousand did turn up for the morning's play. Not that they got much for their rupee – Feroz Shah Kotla was typical of most Indian grounds in that the facilities for the

Say so... "*Ganguly was regularly late for the toss at the start of the Test matches. Steve Waugh didn't say much, but he was far from pleased. To him there was a prescribed time when the game kicked off, and that was that.*"

spectators were almost non-existent. There was one main stand on a couple of levels with the dressing rooms underneath and the rest of the ground was wide open concrete terracing.

The surface of the ground itself was quite good, the pitch absolutely shorn of grass, just rolled mud. I recalled my recent conversation with Bishen Bedi – given the amount of money the Indian Cricket Board have accumulated it seemed extraordinary they couldn't create a more attractive ground for international matches. It was a ground the Australians weren't all that keen on, particularly after their experiences in 1996 when it had turned square from ball one.

Still, this was really an interlude between the main events and little more than an opportunity for some of the players to get the practice that they'd missed out on, given that Australia's batsmen had only had one innings in the Test at Mumbai.

The batsmen seized the opportunity, with a Ponting century in each innings and Mark Waugh an elegant 164, against an underwhelming attack on that grey slab of a pitch offering very little to the bowlers. Somehow the Australians managed to bowl out their opposition for 221, but the match ended in a desultory draw.

The main point of interest at Feroz Shah Kotla was skipper Sourav Ganguly's participation, such as it was.

His only innings produced a near-miss in the first over and eventually a scratchy 40. More noticeably, on the morning of the last day he ambled on to the field some 40 minutes after play had started, and didn't take to the field at all after lunch.

It was an early sign of an attitude that attracted more and more publicity, a good deal of it back in Australia, when it was reported later on that he was regularly late for the toss at the start of the Test matches, keeping Steve Waugh and the umpires waiting.

Waugh didn't say much, but he was far from pleased. To him there was a prescribed time when the toss took place, and that was that. Cammie Smith, the match referee, had to tick the Indian captain off for it, but Ganguly fobbed him off by saying he had a lot of other commitments and just couldn't get there on time.

The truth is there were times when he was just blatantly discourteous and disrespectful to his opponents, and maybe to his own team.

OK, he's a fairly haughty fellow. Perhaps he's a bit of a throwback to the old days of Indian cricket. He

Truly Ganguly

The Indian captain, whose private life was examined daily by the local tabloids, was notoriously involved in a dalliance with a glamorous film star called Nagma, and as Ganguly was married, the scandal was beaten up to ever more epic proportions. Fuel was added to the outrage by the news that Ganguly had decided to stay at a different Delhi hotel from his team-mates. While they made do with fairly modest accommodation, he had checked into the five-star Taj, where the Australian team were also staying.

In a story headlined "Maharaja and His Subjects" one paper made much of the fact that Ganguly was the scion of a wealthy printing family in Calcutta and infamous for his aloofness.

In another gossip sheet the following imaginary conversation between the lovers was "overheard" in a restaurant:

Nagma: "You made one run in the second innings."
Sourav: "I got run out because of you. But then, I was not run out, I was actually lbw."
Nagma: "You mean leg before wicket."
Sourav: "No, Lover Besides Wife. I was actually thinking of running around the trees with you and singing a duet. Of course, before I got married to Dona, lbw meant Love Before Wedding .."

There was also a tale, perhaps apocryphal, that he had once toured with a youth team to Australia and had refused to act as twelfth man in one game, saying, "I don't carry drinks for anyone."

comes from a comfortable background and he's got to a position of some influence.

None of that was an excuse during the Test series. He set a bad example to his team, and in the way he conveyed himself to the opposition.

On the other hand, there was certainly a competitive edge and a toughness about him that shouldn't be underestimated. I'm sure the Australians in their own subtle way let him know what they thought about him and his lady friend – he was probably copping a little of what Steve Waugh calls "mental disintegration". But he stood up to that pretty well. And as the series progressed he could take some credit for the steeliness that India showed, no doubt helped by coach John Wright's influence in the dressing room.

It's a bit hard to evaluate Ganguly because his own form suffered during the series, and any leader wants to be in the position where he's got respect for his own performances. He frankly didn't contribute very much with the bat, and there were times when it looked as though the pressure of quality bowling had got to him. And yet there were other times, as we were to see in Calcutta, where he batted long enough to see his side into a position where a partnership could be created.

As for personal issues between the captains or the players, I don't think there's much to that.

Though on his return to Australia Steve Waugh was asked for a no-nonsense comment on Ganguly by Ian Healy at the NSW end-of-season presentation night.

Waugh's summation: "He's a prick – and that's paying him a compliment."

After the first day's cricket between Australia and the Board President's XI, I took a ride back into town to have a look at some of the life in the middle of Delhi. Connaught Place is a huge area of colonnaded shops, and to the side of it there's an underground emporium festooned with shops selling all sorts of craft, leather, jewellery, CDs, you name it – all the bric-a-brac a

Say so... *"You were very, very lucky," a voice said in my ear.*

"Very lucky — that could have landed on your clothes or your head."

I found myself staring into the concerned brown eyes of a shoe shine man.

tourist might be inclined to throw his money at, or at least be willing to haggle for.

You can get into all sorts of trouble in a place like this, particularly when you emerge unsuspectingly as I did and all of a sudden feel a large dollop of something land on your shoe.

"You were very, very lucky," a voice said in my ear. "Very lucky – that could have landed on your clothes or your head."

I found myself staring into the concerned brown eyes of a shoe shine man. He in turn contemplated the dollop on my shoe and said brightly, "I will fix up this accident. I will fix up this misfortune for you."

Which he did, removing the shoe before I could stop him and sitting me down. There were a few people around who I thought looked a little amused about what was going on, but it was happening too fast to stop, with the shoe shine man insisting this was a dreadful smell, this bird stuff on your shoe. "Terrible, terrible to get off," he said.

As he started working away at one of the shoes and giving it a sparkle, a mate turned up with a little box and a thimble and cotton, and started poking around in the other shoe. He discovered that, yes, there was a problem with that. Sadly, it had some stitching missing, but fortunately this could be fixed too. And away he went to work.

They beavered away there for about 10 minutes, repairing and polishing, stitching and shining, two young hustlers in action.

At the end of it, I pulled out a 100 rupee note, thinking that would be a sufficient reward.

A day or two earlier in Mumbai, I'd been asked by a young boy who had befriended me on a walk around the streets for two rupees for a shoe polish, so I had an idea of the going rate. A hundred was plenty. However, there was great agitation at this.

"Oh, no, no, no, no," said the guy who'd cleaned the shoe. "475 rupees, that is the going price for this work. A very messy work ..." And on he went.

I protested at the excessive price, and he said he'd front me up to his boss, or something like that, and before I knew it a few other men, probably mates, gathered round and the discussion got bigger. Someone thought 350 might be a fair price, but even so the haggling went on.

I was clearly being taken for a ride, but just to get away from it all I gave each of the guys 200 rupees, which was an extortionate amount, I knew that, and I made my getaway.

Once I'd shaken them off, I was continuing around Connaught Place when another young man came up to me, wanting me to hire one of the tuk-tuks at the roadside. I refused but he was persistent, with the usual "I only learn English from talking to foreigners, I don't want to take money from you." As he walked beside me, he noticed that my shoes were very, very clean.

Say so... *"That's a very old trick, very old trick," I was told by the young man in the street. I didn't tell him how much I'd paid the two hustlers who had relieved me of 400 rupees — but I had been decidedly had.*

"A shoe shine man has obviously been doing some good work on your shoes, sir."

So I told him the story and he said, "That's a very old trick, very old trick, played on all the foreigners who come here. That not bird s***, that cow s***. One of these men has gone on one side of you to distract you, and the other fellow's gone the other side and dropped the cow s*** straight on your shoe."

I didn't tell him how much I'd paid, because I had been decidedly had. There was nothing to be done but retain some sense of humour. Bird s***, indeed!

Given their prevalence in India, I thought, it's a good thing cows don't fly.

Did I Really Say That?

COMING TO YOU LIVE ... AN IDIOT AT THE MIKE

On air foot-in-mouth disease, there's always an opportunity for that. I wouldn't claim to be in the same league as English commentator Brian Johnston, whose "the bowler's Holding the batsman's Willey" and "so it's Lillee caught Willey bowled Dilley" are legendary.

Brian had a wonderful sense of humour and I suspect he contrived a few, and just waited for his opportunity.

One Maxwell-ism I do remember was on the last day of the Boxing Day Test against England in Melbourne in 1982-83.

The game was basically all over going into the fourth day, with Australia needing another 70 to win but only Border and Jeff Thomson remaining with one wicket in hand. With the game likely to finish with any one ball, the authorities decided on the final morning to let the crowd in for nothing.

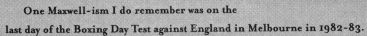

THE TENSION WAS BUILDING UP AND MY FOCUS WAS ON THE MATCH. I DIDN'T EVEN KNOW I'D SAID ANYTHING STUPID AT THE TIME...

Still, there must have been 20,000 people in there for the action, and the game went on for the best part of an hour as Thomson and Border kept making runs and creeping ever closer to the target.

The tension was building up and the crowd was very animated and my focus was on the match at hand. I didn't even know I'd said anything stupid at the time.

Without thinking, I said, "Well, the crowd that's been let in free today are really getting their money's worth ... and now Willis comes in again to bowl ..."

About five minutes later our producer, Clark Hansen, appeared in the box and tapped me on the shoulder.

"A bloke has just rung up about something you said a moment ago ..."

I never lived it down.

As for the match, there was no fairytale ending. Thomson finally got out and England won by a handful of runs.

Calcutta

THE AUSTRALIAN JUGGERNAUT SEEMED
UNSTOPPABLE, WITH YET ANOTHER VICTORY
BECKONING AT THE HALFWAY MARK OF
THE SECOND TEST. BUT THIS WAS INDIA,
WHERE STRANGE THINGS CAN HAPPEN.

W left Delhi in the early evening, literally shaking the city's ubiquitous fine red dust off our feet as we boarded our spick Jet Airlines aircraft for the two-hour hop to Calcutta. For many years Indian Airlines had a monopoly over the airline traffic but in the last few years there have been competitive new players, such as Jet Airlines.

I must say they could teach our own domestic airlines a few tricks in terms of the presentation. It's the little things, like the genuine cotton napkins.

There was a choice of vegetarian or non-vegetarian, of course, and I enjoyed a very mild curry with lentils and spices, followed by a dessert that tasted like a subtle custard with coconut.

It was all quite delicious, and delightfully served by the attractive flight attendants.

Seeing the women in those magnificently colourful saris everywhere in India it is no wonder that country has produced so many Miss Worlds.

At Calcutta we were greeted by a wonderful sight – a gleaming, white, air-conditioned Mercedes waiting to take us to the Oberoi Grand Hotel.

We appreciated the comfort on the 40-minute drive through the night traffic, weaving among rickshaws and bicycles, the air so heavy with smog that the headlights of oncoming vehicles cast shafts of light through the suspended particles of pollution.

Magnificent saris, colourful and richly patterned, were everywhere to be seen in India. Even the cleaning staff at the stadium looked splendid in their finery..

Many things go on behind the scenes when you're covering sport in another country, and sometimes there are misunderstandings that very nearly go to air by mistake. Soon after arriving in Calcutta, the now infamous Slater-Dravid brouhaha hit the top of the agenda once again with the news that Michael Slater had made comments on a radio station at home, despite having been told, as I'd heard it, to keep his mouth shut or risk further trouble because of his outspokenness.

As a result, a call came through for me from the ABC in Australia. They had received a wire story from

Associated Press with the "news" that Slater had been suspended for the next match. I was asked for a reaction piece, which I did on the spot, saying how surprising it was for Slater to receive this one-match suspension, but perhaps, in view of what occurred at the time, it may have been the penalty he should have copped in the first place.

Later on, having done the story and while talking about who would take Slater's place, I began to get an uneasy feeling. I had an instinct, call it experience, that there was something awry in all of this.

So I rang Brian Murgatroyd, the Australian team's media liaison man.

"No, no, no, they've got it all wrong," Brian told me. "He's got a suspended one-match suspension for

Temper, temper!

I think at times the players forget they're on centre stage and that any moment of rancour on field will be picked up and magnified by the press.

In that sense the Australian players have been more fortunate than their English counterparts, because of the more competitive nature of the UK media. The English players tend to get torn apart for any indiscretion either on or off the field.

Ian Botham was done over a number of times, but his outrageous behaviour was perhaps intended to attract the publicity. That's the nature of the man. Some people go out looking for it.

Dennis Lillee did at times, I'm sure. He was a showman. People who put themselves in that position have got to take care, because if they don't get it right they're going to get hammered.

The infamous Lillee-Miandad incident in Perth was a classic case of it,

and both players were fortunate they didn't cop a more severe penalty. During the 1981-82 series, in the Perth Test match, Dennis Lillee had impeded Pakistan's Javed Miandad during a run and there'd obviously been an exchange of words — there often was when Miandad was around. It got pretty heated and ended up with Miandad raising his bat at the bowler and Lillee trying to kick him. Umpire Tony Crafter had to intervene.

Lillee just lost it. I can remember at the time, Alan McGilvray and Bill O'Reilly reacted strongly, both of them saying that he should be banned. Where many people saw it as merely a lapse on Lillee's part, the old brigade were really taken aback. Over a number of beers at the end of the day, they expressed the forceful view that he should be banned for life, never allowed to play again.

In the end he got off pretty lightly with a $200 fine that was later beefed up on the next six months, not an immediate one-match suspension, plus a 50 per cent match fine."

I hung up and immediately rang Australia. It was very early in the morning at home, and the piece hadn't gone to air. I was able to redo the whole yarn, getting the facts right this time. One of those narrow escapes.

As for Michael Slater himself, he appeared not to be too pleased with the treatment he was receiving. Perhaps he was in a state of denial.

Eden Gardens, the Calcutta cricket ground, is perhaps the biggest in the world when it's full. Its terracing starts at the edge of the ground and goes far back on a couple of levels, not as steeply as the MCG, but sufficient to hold over 100,000 spectators. We knew that there were

appeal to a two-match suspension. Just a slap on the wrist. Miandad's defence was provocation, saying that Lillee had been abusing him constantly — "mimicking, clapping derisively and sitting on the pitch" was the official Pakistan complaint.

McGilvray's reaction soured his relationship with Dennis Lillee. It was the year of Lillee's testimonial and McGilvray had been invited that night to a celebratory dinner. He didn't go. Mac was in high dudgeon.

It was a regrettable incident but I don't think Dennis realised at the time how bad it looked on television. And he's certainly not the only offender over the years.

Think of Ian Healy's act of dissent when he threw the bat into the dressing room from outside the door and the TV camera happened to pick it up.

And there was Rodney Hogg in Melbourne years ago, technically run out after defending the ball and then stepping outside his crease. Because the ball wasn't dead when the fieldsman picked the ball up, he was able to be run out. Hogg was so incensed he turned around and smashed the stumps down. I think that was a pretty fair reaction, quite understandable.

It makes you wonder what used to happen in pre-television days when such incidents occurred on the field. Unless — snap! — a photographer got the exact moment, there must have been plenty that no one ever knew about.

You do get the impression that overall it was a more gentlemanly game than it is today. It's far more confrontational in every aspect because there's more at stake. I think there has to be some room for theatre on the ground, as long as it doesn't boil over. That's why limits will always be needed. It's like disciplining your children — there are boundaries, aren't there, boundaries of behaviour that you must stick within.

going to be a lot of people there, and because there have been riots at this ground in recent years, notably in 1999 when the final day of the Indian/Pakistan match had to be played before an empty house as a result, there was going to be a huge security presence.

There were in fact 8000 of them. It was an awesome sight, the traffic policemen in white, the regular policemen in khaki, and the special police in their model blue and white that reminded me of the Nepalese police I'd encountered on a previous visit to India. Some were even on horseback, and all of them carried the familiar long wooden lathi sticks and oval-shaped cane shields.

Outside the ground the crowds were corralled in bamboo races that had been specially constructed to channel them through the correct gates. It was all quite effective, but it did have the look of something better suited to managing cattle or sheep than people.

Our initial problem was just going to be getting into the ground. All the touring journalists and broadcasters already had security clearance, but here, we learnt, this was not sufficient. We'd need to get another pass, the one issued for the whole series wasn't good enough.

Say so... *"An important Hindu festival made it impossible to get help. It meant, horror of horrors, the Second Test began with the ABC commentary team once more doing the best we could by passing the mobile phone around the box."*

On a hot, crowded and frustrating day of pre-match tension – yes, you guessed it, we had technical problems and were waiting for "the man" again – this was not the sort of hassle I needed, and I can remember having a heated discussion with Mr Ghosh, one of the assistant-joint-secretaries, of which there appeared to be several at the Calcutta Cricket Club.

Eventually he pointed me in the direction of All India Radio and there, as so often in India, I found myself talking to someone across a desk while six other conversations were going on in the same room. It was as if everyone had to be in the presence of someone

124

with authority. Whether it was the Assistant Director of All India Radio, another Mr Ghosh, or someone else in the cricket hierarchy that you had go and see, the hangers-on were always there, all crammed into the room, all having their say. It was chaos.

Anyway, not without further difficulty, I got what I needed. The next challenge was to get through the security cordon.

After the saga of Mumbai, I won't burden you with further tales of the technical problems we had in setting up the broadcast. Sufficient to say they involved the local telephone company, a helpful but ineffectual Mr Chaudry who could get us the lines but apparently not the right connection, long and noisy discussions about voltage quality, not to mention the added complications of Holi Day, or "Colour Day".

A highlight of this significant Hindu festival, which marks the end of winter, is that people hurl coloured water bombs at each other and daub themselves – and sometimes unwary passers-by – with red, blue and pink colouring. We also saw quite a few people high on a drink called "bhang lassi", a combination of milk and the ground leaves of cannabis.

Unfortunately for us, Holi Day coincided with our efforts to set up the commentary lines, and with everything throughout the city closed, trying to chase people up was impossible.

It meant, horror of horrors, that the Second Test began with the ABC commentary team once more doing the best we could by passing the mobile phone around the box. I thought it was brilliantly accomplished, though I'm not sure the feeling was shared back home by the ABC management.

The cavalry was on its way, however, thanks to the intervention of Mr Manoj, an Indian plastic surgeon. He enabled us to find a number that Sydney could ring so that we could get the equipment up and working. After that we were fine.

We were fortunate that this happened in time for us to provide proper coverage of an amazing hat-trick by off-spinner Harbhajan Singh, the first by an Indian in

You weren't allowed to carry anything but yourself inside the Eden Gardens ground in Calcutta. The wording on the back of the ticket said it all:
"Must be produced at the gate for readmission. Ticket must be checked whenever required. Transistor radio, camera, video camera, metal boxes, mirror, any kind of bottle including plastic bottle, will not be allowed inside the stadium. For your assistance, do not carry fire crackers inside the ground, do not set waste paper or inflammable materials to fire in the galleries, do not throw any missile like oranges etc inside the ground, drinking alcohol inside the stadium is strictly prohibited, do not rush inside the ground even after the game is concluded..."

Where are yer glasses, Ump?

....

IT'S TIME TO REWRITE THE RULES FOR UMPIRES.

Is there a cricket fan in the world who doesn't have an opinion about umpires? What a job — you'd have to wonder sometimes why anybody wants to do it.

Everyone makes mistakes, but what the game demands is that umpires make them less often. We've had too many incompetents for too long, and the forensic analysis of television replay has shown up the umpires who are nowhere near the game.

There are a couple of things to be said here.

First, there's the whole concept of independent umpires, and getting the structure in place to pay them. The ICC have empanelled an elite international group of eight top men. How they choose these eight without arousing all kinds of national unrest remains to be seen.

Secondly, there is the question of match referees. (The match referee is the one who sits over the whole game and adjudicates on all the things that aren't able to be dealt with immediately, including Code of Conduct issues.)

While there are a couple of very good match referees, such as Mike Denness and Peter Burge, some of the others are there as reward for long service to their cricket boards. It has become a real old boys club — "incompetent" is the word that comes to mind. We badly need a younger group of referees, some of whom are perhaps bowlers and not batsmen.

Given this current state of affairs, could technology provide an answer? My opinion is that umpiring should be left to the men in the middle as much as possible. Clearly on matters of fact like run-outs and stumpings, it's worth referring to the third umpire. If you're going to give the audience conclusive evidence on whether a batsman's out or not out, and you're going to deny that evidence to the arbiters, then you've got a problem.

So let's go for better umpires, and give them the power. I believe it's an imperative on the captains in this era to tell the ICC what's needed — that they're prepared to invest more power in the men in the middle providing we're given the most competent officials.

If we're given that, players and fans alike will wear the occasional mistake.

As a postscript, I was once asked what was the worst example of umpiring incompetence I've seen. The most galling, I think, was in a Test match in the West Indies in '91. Local umpire Lloyd Barker gave Geoff Marsh out lbw in the second innings when the ball would have missed the leg stump by six inches at least. It got the West Indies on a roll at a time when the game was still wide open, and could be said to have changed the course of the match. It was a shocker.

Say so... *"You can imagine the pandemonium in the stadium. Harbhajan Singh had taken his hat-trick and at that moment was the most popular man at Eden Gardens, if not the entire nation of over a billion people."*

the history of Test cricket – the first hat-trick in 338 Tests that India had been involved in. It was a remarkable event and deserves recalling in some detail.

It was after tea on the first day, Australia were batting and heading towards a big score, when Harbhajan Singh took his first wicket. Ponting was lbw, a straightforward enough decision for umpire Bansal, going across his stumps and missing the ball while trying to hit to the on side.

The next ball, to the new batsman Gilchrist, was more dubious. It looked like it pitched outside the leg stump, Gilchrist may also have nicked it into his pads, but Bansal, officiating in his last Test match, quickly fired him out.

And then came the third one, Shane Warne prodding forward. There was no doubt that Ramesh at short leg took a brilliant one-handed catch with his right hand; the big question was whether it was hit on the full or was a bump ball. For some strange reason umpire Bansal called for the help of the third umpire.

Now, if you know the rules that apply to the third umpire and the limitations placed on his role, you know that he is only permitted to adjudicate on whether the ball has carried on the full – he can't make any judgment on what it has done immediately after leaving the bat. So it did seem a pretty superfluous exercise.

Maybe the umpire should have given Warne out straight away if he was convinced that the fielder had taken it on the full.

Anyway, after deliberation and the evidence of one quality angle showing the interception had been indeed been made on the full, the hat-trick was given.

You can imagine the pandemonium in the stadium. Harbhajan Singh, the 20-year-old from the Punjab, was

It's a first-class world now for the players. They're well looked after, stay in five-star hotels, and just about everything is done for them. How things have changed. Neil Harvey told me that when they went to India in the 1950s most of the boys only ate bananas and boiled eggs. They were too scared to touch anything else.

They would have stayed at much lesser hotels than today, of course, and there may not have been much Western food available.

But the fact is there's no longer the kind of phobia about going to the subcontinent there used to be. A few of the players welcome the chance to immerse themselves in another culture.

Justin Langer and Steve Waugh in particular always seize the opportunity to extend themselves beyond the cricket. Steve's support of the orphan girls at the Udayan leper colony near Calcutta is typical.

And he's not just playing to the crowd to get brownie points. He's genuine about it, as he is about so many things.

at that moment the most popular man at Eden Gardens, if not the entire nation of over a billion people

Following this spectacular collapse, Australia struggled to the end of the day at 8-291, still a healthy score. They resumed on the second day at 8-291, with Steve Waugh on 29 and Gillespie on six.

An early end to the innings might have been in Indian minds, but it wasn't to be. Gillespie's long reach and excellent temperament helped the combative Waugh add a record 133 for the ninth wicket, extending the innings past lunch.

Gillespie was out for a Test-best 46. Last man McGrath came out to join his captain, and stayed around long enough to see Steve reach his 25th Test century, his first in India.

The Bengali crowd of 75,000 applauded generously, giving a standing ovation to a man popular not only for his indomitable skill, but also for his humanity in continuing to support his "daughters", the leper orphan children at Udayan, whom he had visited on the day before the match. He repeatedly saluted the crowd with his arms and bat raised high. In return, they accorded him a standing and thunderous ovation.

Soon afterwards Waugh was the last man out, lbw on the sweep to Harbhajan for 110, while McGrath remained 21 not out.

Australia's last two wickets had added 176 runs, guiding the tourists to a total of 445. Harbhajan Singh finished with 7/123 from his 37.5 overs.

India's innings began disastrously, with Ramesh falling to Gillespie in the second over, before a run had been scored. At tea they were 1-32, and afterwards we witnessed a swarming Australian effort in the field, highlighted by McGrath's third-ball dismissal of Tendulkar, plumb lbw to an inswinger.

While his arrival at the crease had been greeted with delirious cheers, his departure was met with almost stunned silence. India capitulated. They were 8-128 at

Say so... "*I picked up a bargain, a sandalwood carving of Ganesha, the Hindu elephant god who is said to be the remover of obstacles. Mr Subramanian had faith in his power — we reckoned any assistance in the box was welcome.*"

stumps, trailing by 317 runs and still requiring a further 118 to avoid the follow-on.

Glenn and I talked about the probability of another three-day Test match as we walked back to the hotel in the fading light, amid the bus fumes and food stalls, the magicians and ticket touts offering bargain bus trips to Darjeeling. With all our equipment in tow, we were obviously tourists in need of guidance.

I had dinner that night with some of the Channel Nine guys, and I also picked up a bargain: a sandalwood carving of Ganesha, the Hindu elephant god who is said to be the remover of obstacles.

Mr Subramanian had faith in Ganesha's power – that morning he had propped a little plastic card bearing the god's image on the phone equipment in our commentary box. Both Glenn and I approved – we reckoned any assistance was welcome! The statue set me back 1600 rupees ($A68), hopefully a small price to pay for putting all our obstacles behind us.

And indeed, Mr Subramnian and Ganesha were to join forces in a memorable way, but that's a story for later on and the final dramatic match at Chennai.

Next morning, right on nine o'clock, an air-raid-like siren blared out over the city to remind everyone that it was time to be at work. Half an hour later, the cricketers too, were back at work.

Within an hour India had lost their last two wickets and were dismissed for 171, a deficit of 274 runs. They were asked to follow on.

During the change in innings, I interviewed Jagmohan Dalmiya, the immediate past president of the ICC and the current head of the Cricket Association of Bengal. Some reports had linked his name to corruption in the game, and in particular to the deals on television rights. He was impeccably dressed, with not a crease in his beige safari suit, immaculate shiny shoes, a diamond-studded gold Rolex watch and a ring that boasted an enormous diamond. Obviously the construction business has treated him well.

In the follow-on, India announced a change in the batting order. The man from Hyderabad with the resonant name, Vangipurapu Venkata Sai Laxman, was promoted to number three in place of the out-of-form Dravid. Laxman, whom many Sydneysiders remembered for his enthralling innings of 169 during the 1999-2000 tour of Australia, had been the last man out in the first innings for 59.

Soon after lunch, with the score at 52, India lost their first wicket, that of Ramesh. Laxman joined Das, and began with a stirring off-driven four. It was a portent, but not one that any of us in the commentary box could have spotted.

The only signs we could see were ominous ones for India – Harsha Bhogle was so anxious he spoke into the microphone, with both hands tightly wrapped around the little Ganesha statue, in the hope that it would remove his team's obstacles.

Say so... "*As Tendulkar made his way back to the Indian dressing room, a disgruntled fan hurled a water pouch in his direction. The police mobilised. Such behaviour towards the god–like batsman was akin to sacrilege.*"

Soon Das was pushed back by Gillespie's pace and trod on his wicket. An unsettled Tendulkar wafted ineffectually at a ball from Gillespie and Gilchrist took the catch behind.

The locals were getting restless as well. As Tendulkar crossed the rope and on to the lawn in front of the Indian dressing room, a disgruntled fan hurled a water pouch in his direction.

This quickly mobilised a large group of police, who with the aid of the spectators, were guided to the offender, who was promptly marched away.

Harsha Bhogle, commentating at the time, said that

Say so... *"Laxman, swashbuckling yet controlled, counterattacked. Many of his first 100 runs came from Warne, whose around–the–wicket tactic was confounded by footwork that Warne described as the best he could remember."*

most Indians would see such behaviour towards the god-like Tendulkar as being akin to sacrilege.

Things were looking bleak for the home side. India were 3-115 and facing the prospect of their third consecutive under-three-day loss to Australia.

You may recall that back home I'd been given odds of 20-1 on a three-nil series whitewash by Australia. So I was in good shape. It was round about now that I made that most elemental of punter's errors – I mentally started to count my future winnings.

Meanwhile we all turned our attention to the incoming batsman, captain Sourav Ganguly, and his surviving partner, Laxman.

Ganguly's arrival at the wicket was given a rather muted reception, considering his normally exalted status here in Calcutta. Steve Waugh really went on the attack, with a mocking bowling tactic from Kasprowicz. He placed every fieldsman on the offside, an act that smacked of contempt, and of Waugh's belief that Ganguly was sure to play another "I don't want to be here" stroke.

As I mentioned earlier, Ganguly, the local favourite, or prince of Bengal, had not impressed the Australians. However, on this third day in Calcutta, Ganguly was defiant. And Laxman, swashbuckling yet controlled, counterattacked. His driving was powerful and decisive, without any hint of risk. Seventy per cent of his first 100 runs were scored through the onside, many from Warne, whose around-the-wicket tactic was confounded by footwork that Warne would later describe as the best he could remember.

Laxman and Ganguly added 117, until McGrath's perseverance around the wicket produced a Ganguly snick. Regular number three, Dravid, joined Laxman 35 minutes before stumps. Bowled easily by Warne in the first innings, he looked determined to make amends. He saw Laxman through to his century, and stumps, at 4-254, with India now only 20 in arrears.

It had been a terrific fightback, but they were a long way from getting out of the woods. At the media conference, Laxman was upbeat. He felt that if India could get a lead of 225, they could provide Australia with some problems.

Rupees for Runs

By stumps, India had gone through the day without losing a wicket and had effectively put an end to Australia's 16-Test winning streak.

Laxman was unbeaten on 275, the fourth highest score by anyone against Australia, bettered only by Len Hutton's 364, RE Foster's 287 and Brian Lara's 277. He had also surpassed Rohan Kanhai's 256 in 1958-59, the previous highest Test score on Indian soil, which coincidentally was also made on this ground. It was a remarkable innings in which he never offered a chance.

Dravid reached stumps on 155. Their partnership stood at 357, with 335 of those runs being added on the fourth day. The lead was 315 as the total stood at 4/589.

For Warne in particular it was another dark day at Eden Gardens. Three years earlier he had returned his worst figures in a Test innings, sending down 42 overs for 0/147. He finished this day with 1/152.

In an act that was peculiarly Indian, Laxman's innings was honoured during the tea interval. The large electronic scoreboard carried a message from the Cricket Association of Bengal, which outlined a monetary reward scheme for Laxman. He was to receive 200,000 rupees for having made 200, a further 1000 rupees for every run he scored between 200 and 236 and then 2000 rupees for each run beyond 237. By stumps, his score had resulted in him pocketing a cool 312,000 rupees, about $A13,000.

The CAB also decided to award 100,000 rupees ($A4200) to Harbhajan Singh for his first-day hat-trick. In addition, the Indian team would share in a 500,000 rupees ($A20,800) bonus if they could win the match.

The government of West Bengal had also jumped on the bandwagon, offering a further 100,000 rupees each to Laxman and Harbhajan.

Say so... *"It had been a terrific fightback, but India were not yet out of the woods. Before play next morning, Mr Subramanian placed a red tilak mark on the forehead of the Ganesha statue. I guess he thought every little bit helps."*

For their part, the Australians were confident that one breakthrough would suffice to create a collapse. They had bowled all day with an expectation of dismissing him, thinking as it went on that this couldn't last. Most of us would have agreed.

Come the morning, it was said, and Gillespie and McGrath would break the partnership, and they had a second new ball to almost guarantee that wicket. Almost. Not quite.

Once again Glenn and I walked back to the Oberoi Grand, where we dined early in La Terrasse restaurant.

Before play next morning, Mr Subramanian placed a red tilak mark on the forehead of the Ganesha statue. I guess he thought every little bit helps.

It was an almost unbearably hot day, the most humid so far in Calcutta, and it provided the sweltering backdrop against which India staged one of the great Test fightbacks.

Neither Laxman nor Dravid offered a chance that day. I counted three miscues from the Hyderabadi stylist: two inside edges, and one snick to a vacant second slip. A measure of Laxman's ability to hit fours, taking occasional leisurely singles, was his 200 subscript: 35 fours, 31 singles. Waugh tried nine bowlers, and Ponting bowled as well as any of them, going within a centimetre of claiming an lbw verdict against Dravid in the last over before lunch.

Dravid's support for Laxman was magnificent, finding his confidence and range of piercing shots, as the partnership reached 357 at stumps on the fourth day. India's total was 4-589, a lead of 315.

Both batsmen laboured with cramp in the final session, but they were committed, and driven by a boisterous, regaling crowd that again touched 70,000. Laxman raced past Sunil Gavaskar's record 236, and ended the day unbeaten on 275. He and Dravid, not out on 155, recovered on saline drips at day's end, while a revitalised Ganguly pondered over the timing of a declaration.

To their credit, the Australians took things in a very sportsmanlike fashion with each milestone greeted with warm applause and congratulations.

The crowd at times was at fever pitch. As both batsmen left the field, all their team-mates came down to the boundary rope to cheer them off.

The haunting sound of Calcutta's nine o'clock siren, clocking-on time for the city's workforce, blasted forebodingly on the final morning.

Aiming for his 43rd four, Laxman was caught at point after almost 11 hours of wonderful batting, and a partnership of 376 that was the highest for the fifth wicket by any team against Australia.

Australia were set an improbable 384 to win from 75 overs when Ganguly closed at eight for 657, a total that precisely equalled the highest by a team forced to follow on – Pakistan at Bridgetown in 1957-58.

A draw was the most likely result, but the prospect of losing became a nightmare that steadily, inexorably, took on the shape of reality for Australia.

As Hayden and Slater established themselves in an opening stand worth 74, off-spinner Harbhajan hit Slater in the chest with one viciously bouncing delivery, a portent of the trouble ahead. Ganguly grabbed a close-in catch, Langer's sweeping tactics failed, and Mark Waugh fell to Raju's arm ball; the first of five lbw decisions given by umpire Bansal in his swansong Test.

Ganguly spilt a chance from Steve Waugh at 3-127, but when Bedani snapped up another offering just after tea, Waugh's departing solemnity looked fatalistic.

Ponting surrendered meekly, Gilchrist swept prematurely, completing a king pair, Hayden missed a fuller delivery on his favourite sweep shot, and Warne failed to read Tendulkar's wrong 'un. Last pair

Danger! Don't look up!

THE FAMOUS CASE OF THE DISAPPEARING TV MONITOR

At the Eden Gardens ground in Calcutta the commentary positions are open to the elements and the action in the crowd.

Our commentary position was above the area in front of the members stand, with a tunnel immediately below us. We were at the end of about four narrow commentary positions, and the one next door to us had a television monitor hanging off the wall.

All of a sudden, at teatime on the last day, with people milling around below, this television set wasn't there any more. The bracket collapsed and the whole lot dropped like a stone into the crowd about four metres below.

A policeman standing below was hit on the shoulder and knocked askew, but it could so easily have been worse. It could have landed on a child, even killed someone.

> "THE BRACKET COLLAPSED AND THE WHOLE LOT DROPPED LIKE A STONE INTO THE CROWD ABOUT FOUR METRES BELOW."

The bad news for us, with the game at a crucial stage and Australia fighting to save a draw, was that this television monitor had been the one we looked at for replays — we'd got rid of our own because of the cramped conditions.

So now we didn't have the replays and our only chance to see them was on a monitor about three boxes away.

Of course, with the game reaching a tremendous climax and the noise in the stadium deafening, there seemed to be one contentious lbw after another in the last session. It's the way things are in India.

Kasprowicz and McGrath resisted stubbornly, until Harbhajan was switched to umpire Bansal's end, and McGrath padded up once too often.

Eden Gardens erupted, many fans lighting pieces of paper and waving them around like Olympic torches at an opening ceremony. The stand was illuminated in the twilight by thousands of bright orange flames. As they burned a pall of smoke drifted across the ground.

The greatest match in the history of Test cricket? It was surely the most amazing recovery to win a Test, inspired by VVS Laxman's flawless, commanding 281. India had won by 171 runs with 5.3 overs to spare. Harbhajan, who took 13 match wickets, was first among 75,000 enthusiasts who applauded Laxman when he was named man of an unforgettable match.

The loss was a shock to Australia. Their batting had been neglectful on the final day, and again they had shown an inability to deal under pressure with the off-spin bowling of Harbhajan.

The Australians felt they'd had the rough end of the pineapple in the decisions in the match, particularly from umpire Bansal on the last day, but in fact it was hard to fault most of them. There was a little bit of maybe about the final lbw, but McGrath himself knew that padding up to a ball near the line of the off stump was asking for trouble. The Australian players should have seen the likely outcome as soon as Ganguly switched Harbhajan from Peter Willey's end to Bansal's.

Really, it was poor batting. In later conversations it was clear that the Australians hadn't prepared themselves for the difficulty of having to cope with spin. Whereas Laxman had on-driven Shane Warne like no right-hander I had ever seen, the Australians didn't seem to have the answers. They weren't able to use the necessary quick footwork to negate Harbhajan Singh.

It was a question of surprise, and maybe some underestimation of his ability. Langer and Ponting in particular didn't come to terms with his bowling.

VVS – Very, Very Special

....

LAXMAN PROBABLY PLAYED THE INNINGS OF HIS LIFE.

What actually wins matches, bat or ball? In Calcutta you'd have to say the bat of VVS Laxman gave a persuasive answer to that old chestnut.

During his innings, Australia were always bowling with the basic expectation of "one wicket and the game's all over".

Watching and calling the game, that's what all of us felt. India were playing well, but they had only to lose a wicket and they were history. And it didn't happen.

That's the point. In the history of the game, when you get a batsman who can score quickly and so demoralise the bowlers that they're not sure where to bowl, he has to be at least as significant a force in the outcome of the game as a good bowler.

> "WE ALL FELT INDIA HAD ONLY TO LOSE A WICKET AND THEY WERE HISTORY. AND IT DIDN'T HAPPEN."

Given that when batting the next ball could be your last, it's little short of miraculous how some of the great innings are played. A bowler can be hit for five sixes and still take a hat-trick. A batsman makes one mistake and he's gone.

I think there's another point worth making here about the positive influence that one-day cricket has had for both codes of cricket. Constantly challenged by the pressures of the shorter form of the game, batsmen are no longer just hanging around at the crease and pushing the ball here and there. Things happen electrically – people are getting out or people are getting runs. They're stretched by the game, and they want to dominate.

Laxman's innings was just amazing. OK, he had the force of the world, his own world as it were, behind him. That helped.

In addition, he was in conditions he was familiar with, on a ground that was like a billiard table, so that obviously made a difference too. The raw statistics of his innings provide evidence about the fast outfield and the fact that any good shot that beat the infield was gone for four.

These conditions gave him the confidence to believe that if he just kept his composure and waited for the right opportunity, his rate of scoring would be maintained. But it was still a remarkable innings. Laxman had a belief in his ability to dominate and to control the game - the evidence of his success will be there in the record books for the rest of time.

Chennai

THE SERIES THAT HAD LOOKED LIKE AN
AUSTRALIAN WALKOVER WAS NOW LEVELLED,
AND PULSATING WITH TENSION. THE CARAVAN
MOVED TO THE SOUTHERN CITY OF CHENNAI
WITH THE CERTAINTY OF A RESULT.

With only three days' break between the Second Test and the final encounter at Chennai, formerly known as Madras, neither players nor commentators had time to draw breath.

Calcutta had drained us all, and the strain of the loss was showing in the Australian camp.

Shane Warne was at the centre of the most visible tension. The real disappointment of the Second Test had been Warne's bowling. The Indian batsmen had got to Warney. It's rare that that happens, and I don't think he handled it very well. Against Laxman he wasn't sure whether to bowl leg stump, off stump or wherever, and as a result he got pretty ragged and was picked off. He also failed to get much bounce out of the pitch, even though there was plenty on occasions for Harbhajan Singh, who had – I still don't know how – managed to get one ball to hit Michael Slater in the sternum.

Coach John Buchanan gave an interview in which he hinted that he thought Warne was physically and mentally overwrought following his disappointing 1/152 in the Calcutta Test. For "overwrought" we took it that he was really hinting that Warne might, or even should, be left out of the team for the Final Test.

This was big news, and of course ABC Radio and the newspapers ran strongly with the line. We were soon set straight when Steve Waugh gave us his pre-match chat the next day.

Now, when Steve decides to speak out, you're never going to be left wondering. He was blunt. Certain things to do with the team management, he said, are perhaps "better said within the team than outside". As he was one of the three Test selectors, he left us in no doubt that as far as he was concerned Shane Warne would be playing.

Was it a rebuke to John Buchanan? It was certainly clear that there were different ideas floating around, though how deep the conflict was we could only guess. I'd figured for a while that Buchanan had strong ideas about the personnel he wanted to have around him, and that didn't necessarily include all the people who were involved in the team management at the time. We

On the last morning at Chennai, Mr Subramanian arrived in the box with an assortment of exotica. Two incense sticks went up, which Mr Subramanian lit – a heady element in the enclosed box. Next came flowers, hibiscus and rose petals. He also produced fruit, an orange or two, a tangerine, and then some channa, a savoury chickpea delicacy in a little bowl. All this was in honour of the Hindu god Ganesha, famous for removing obstacles. With the match nearing a tense climax, Mr Subramanian wasn't taking any chances.

wondered, for example, about the position of Steve Bernard, the team manager, Errol Alcott, the team's physiotherapist, and Mike Walsh the assistant manager/scorer. It was as if the team's success had brought John a large slice of the power, and he was looking to exercise some of it.

Warne, as you'll imagine, was not especially impressed by these goings-on. In a subsequent remarkable conversation – given that for whatever reason my relationship with Shane Warne was not an especially easy one – he was candid to me about the robotic nature of John Buchanan's style.

In his view, the coach might have brought some new toys in terms of the computer analysis, but he had a tendency to behave like a schoolmaster and the players weren't all that happy about it. It was only because there was such a hard core of experienced elder players

The coach approach

RUMBLING DISCONTENT ABOUT THE AUSTRALIAN TEAM'S COACHING BROUGHT THE ISSUE INTO FOCUS.

The role of the cricket coach has always been important, and increasingly so with the impact of globalisation on the sport.

New Zealander John Wright was the Indian coach during the series, and I think deserved credit for their tougher attitude. They dealt with the typical Australian aggression on the field, and reciprocated.

Wright played in a period when the Australians were very combative on the field and had the kind of personality that this just rolled off. He imbued the Indian players with this approach. Of course, any New Zealander loves to see the Aussies

defeated. I did a couple of two-way radio broadcasts with New Zealand during the series and they were salivating at the prospect of Australia getting rolled by India. That is both historical and hysterical – going back to the underarm incident and countless others in the Australia-New Zealand sporting relationship.

In 2001 Australian Richard Pybus took over the Pakistan side from Javed Miandad. It was a second incarnation for him, since he'd had a short go in the same position a few years back when they'd come to Australia. They had lost the series and he was immediately dumped, not in the side that they were able to maintain their poise. As Warne saw it, they were mature enough to accept the aspects of John's philosophy that they thought were of value, reject the rest, and just get on with it.

Maybe they would have been more respectful of a coach with a background in the game as a player, but I think that's being unfair to John Buchanan. He did play first-class cricket, and studied coaching methods in the US before coming back to Australia and establishing himself in Queensland as a very good coach.

When he took over from Geoff Marsh with the Australian team, he had the endorsement of Steve Waugh, who could see something in his methods.

I think there's an underlying text to this story. Warne may have felt he was being singled out, but the real agenda was perhaps to give him a bit of a rev-up for the Test match.

The fact is that he immediately did more to make himself fitter and perhaps rethink his approach to his

surprising given the politics of Pakistani cricket. Pybus will be expected to bring important disciplines and organisational factors to Pakistan, the kind of structure that Javed Miandad wasn't able to provide.

Zimbabwean Duncan Fletcher coaches England, and Australians Doug Whatmore and Bruce Yardley have coached in Sri Lanka. In his day Bob Simpson even coached outside Australia, helping out in India and with county teams in England. And Dennis Lillee has worked with the Madras Rubber Foundation, the big sponsors of a fast-bowling academy in Chennai. It's all about getting teams in the right frame of mind to win, and the teams that want to succeed go looking for the best exponents. You imitate the methods of the best teams.

Coaching methods have shifted in their emphasis. With a highly motivated and experienced group of individuals such as the Australian team, a coach's role is more about mentoring than coaching.

Technical problems have to be addressed, but it should be by somebody who knows, rather like getting a reference from a GP to see a specialist. There have probably been times in the past when coaches were a little protective of their position and didn't want outside interference, but I think there's a maturity about this now.

We're certainly seeing this in NSW where Greg Matthews has been the off-spin coach, Geoff Lawson the fast bowling coach, and John Dyson has been doing work with the batting.

At the moment, with the Australian side such a well established team, they're only tinkering with it. But the time for new methods will come.

cricket. On the outside there was apparent harmony, but on the inside there were rumblings. John Buchanan's contract was scheduled to come up for review at the end of the Ashes tour and it would be interesting to see how things transpired.

Indeed the English newshounds were to make a splash of yet another oddity of the "Buchanan style" in a leaked discussion paper in a few months time.

Whatever else, Steve Waugh's remarks clearly told us who was in charge. And that's the way it should be.

It wasn't all long faces. It rarely is when you're surrounded by the kind of pranksters that cricket seems to throw up. Take our perennial nightmare – the technicalities of setting up the broadcast.

Harsha Bhogle had observed, accurately it seemed, that for once everything would be efficient in the lead-up to the game.

"This is the way it is in the south," he said, "it's so much better organised than in the north." Sure enough,

Say so... "*The commentary box was excellent, air-conditioned and well positioned. Channel Nine were even next door, which meant we could quite easily get power and an effects feed. I should have known things were going too well.*"

a whole day before the match began we actually had our broadcasting lines installed and tested. The commentary box was excellent, air-conditioned and well positioned right behind the wicket and alongside the match referee. Channel Nine were even next door, which meant we could quite easily get power and an effects feed.

I should have known things were going too well. The night before the game, Glenn Mitchell and I were at the hotel in our respective rooms, when the phone rang for Glenn. As he told me, a rapid-fire Indian voice introduced himself as the manager from VSNL,

The Sexiest Voice on Radio

····························

AT HOME IN INDIA OUR OLD MATE IS A SUPERSTAR

The most famous man in India must be Sachin Tendulkar, and a close-run second, believe it or not, would have to be fellow commentator Harsha Bhogle. To be on tour with Harsha at an Indian airport was to be with a superstar. He was always fending off autograph hunters when we were having breakfast in the hotel or on our way out to the ground. Indian fans love to be seen with their heroes — it's as if they're living out some kind of fantasy — and Harsha was often mobbed.

The plus for Glenn Mitchell and me was that doors automatically opened wherever we went with him, and given the ups and downs of getting things done in India he was not just a delightful companion.

We first met some 10 years ago. In the lead-up to the Indian tour of Australia in 1991-92, an audition tape arrived at the ABC from this man with the unusual name and the smooth voice. He wrote that he'd done work on All India Radio, and as they weren't sending anyone to Australia for the tour, he intended to come anyway and hoped to write a few articles to get by. Did we have any work to offer?

We liked the sound of what he had to say, and everything else about him once we'd met, so we used him as the Indian commentator throughout that season.

His career has blossomed since. Given an opportunity on ESPN Star, a cable channel that comes out of Singapore with a footprint up across India into Pakistan and China, Harsha has developed from being a cricket frontman to having his own programme, "Harsha on Line".

During the tour he interviewed most of the leading Australian players, including Steve Waugh, Adam Gilchrist, and Australian official Malcolm Speed.

Because terrestrial television in India is a wasteland and most of the major sport is on pay, Harsha's reach and profile are enormous. His audience could be as big as 100 million or more.

He's extremely good at what he does, with a light way of presenting his subject, and a pleasant, rather studious look on camera. I would imagine that he's doing well in his career — when we were there he had recently bought his own place in Mumbai, a city that is one of the ritziest real estate destinations in the world.

Sensibly, though, while things are going well for now, he knows that his career in televison may not be forever, so he's setting up a management company that draws parallels between cricket and business. He has become a sort of guru of the philosophy of cricket and how it can be applied to business.

It's an inventive career plan for the man described in *The Sydney Morning Herald* as having "the sexiest voice on radio anywhere."

the company that operates all the broadcast lines. There was a problem, the man said, rattling off the words. The box we'd been allocated for our commentary position was required by AC Muttiah, the President of the Board of Control. We'd have to be relocated. In addition, we'd have to come down at 7.30 next morning because, unavoidably, there'd be a problem with the lines. All this would need checking. And all at the last minute. He spoke at speed and obviously had no interest in hearing any of Glenn's objections.

The first I knew about the crisis was when there was a banging on my door and a livid Glenn burst in.

"What are we going to do?" he said, as I tried to grasp the news. "There's only one thing for it," he insisted. "Call Harsha. He'll know what to do."

As I picked up the phone to try to track Harsha Bhogle down, there was a rap on the door. Glenn

The Ponting factor

GIFTED, AGGRESSIVE, IMPATIENT, RICKY PONTING WALKED INTO A MINEFIELD OF INDIAN SPIN ARTISTRY.

Ricky Ponting has had great flashes of brilliance as well as inconsistency in his career. Identified as a talent early on – he was playing for Tasmania at 17 – people recognised he was a player of the future.

He arrived in Test cricket with a flourish, 96 on his first appearance in 1995, and but for a dreadful lbw decision by umpire Kaiser Hyatt, known as the "German hotel" for obvious reasons, he would have got a hundred on debut.

Since then he's had a couple of incarnations in Test cricket.

Ponting always had the look of someone who could dominate the bowling, but he seems to have had recurring problems with his footwork, and often on the tour in India he was off balance.

His bottom hand would come into the shot, he'd played across the line and either miscue up on the offside or lose his balance and be a candidate for lbw.

Also, because he tends to go fairly hard at the ball, he was suspect against spin bowlers. Kumble, as we noticed on the '98 tour, and recently Harbhajan Singh, who gets a great deal of bounce, exploited this weakness. If there's anywhere you need to have a soft technique in playing the ball it's in India.

On the other hand, when he gets it

yanked it open, and there, almost by magic, stood Harsha. Glenn just looked at him.

"What do you want, Harsha?" he said.

Then the penny dropped. That non-stop voice on the phone ... the man from VSNL ... hadn't he sounded vaguely familiar..?

We'd been had. Apparently it was standard practice on tour for Harsha to impersonate somebody, either from a telephone company, or a newspaper, or a production house, and the greater the mayhem the more he enjoyed himself. He got us beautifully.

In the lead-up to the match, the Australian batsmen's technique against the spin bowling was clearly a critical issue. Perhaps it was something that the coach needed to be more aware of. Under John Buchanan, there had been a lot of work on peripheral aspects of the team's

right, when he's in the rhythm and his feet, head and everything else are in unison, he's a tremendous attacking player. He's still at a stage in his career where he could have an extraordinary run and dominate bowlers consistently.

Whether you, or he, believe in star signs or not, he's got the traditional luck of a Sagittarian. He's fortunate to have had the universal backing of his captain.

I think this is one of the great attributes of this Australian side – Steve Waugh has a belief in his players. That's why Ponting was persisted with in the Indian series and Martyn didn't come in. Waugh wanted to stick with someone he believed could do the job, even if it didn't happen all the time.

You could also say Ponting is blessed from the point of view that when a team's doing well it can carry players who may have a temporary loss of form. A team that's losing is more inclined to chop and change.

I don't think it's too harsh to say that on occasions, like Shane Warne, Ponting has shown a streak of immaturity. Maybe they have both been indiscreet, picking the wrong place to have a good time and perhaps losing control – notoriously in Ponting's case in a night club in Calcutta in 1998 and later in an incident at a drinking spot in Sydney's Kings Cross.

Now, in another era as I've observed elsewhere, these lapses probably wouldn't have mattered, but today it's hard for the players to get away with any social misbehaviour. Not that they should, but they're still only human after all.

A lot of the people who criticise them are older and have been around longer – many of them have probably played up as cricket, but perhaps more was needed on the players' skill levels in the nets, in particular in preparation for specific match conditions.

It's like practising with a six iron on the golf range – you can hit 100 balls but if you're not doing it right, you're wasting your time. It's not enough just to go through the motions of having a hit.

It became clear that Steve Waugh had his own ideas in this area. Mike Walsh, Assistant Manager and scorer, whose job it was to organise the team practices, told me that Steve was taking special steps in preparing for the Chennai Test match. In the nets, he deliberately scratched up an area outside the off stump so that he could practise against the ball that came biting out of the rough. This was clearly aimed to combat the way that Harbhajan Singh was bowling.

In the final analysis, if there was to be blame apportioned for Australia's failures during the series, it had to be the handful of batsmen who failed to come to terms with spin.

Justin Langer and Ricky Ponting looked particularly inept against the turning ball. Langer, for instance, seemed to operate a "numbers" policy, taking the view that he'd just play a predetermined sweep shot. More often than not he was miscuing or missing.

Ponting seemed to be sweeping on length, no matter what the line. In contrast, Matthew Hayden was playing with considerable skill, either padding, lapping the ball or slog-sweeping in front or square. His method had been wholly successful and the question was why

much as these guys do, but they're not in the public eye in the same way.

On and off the field, I think there have been moments when Ponting has had that rush of blood, a kind of white line fever. On the field we've noticed he's gone over the top at times, and shown a lack of respect for his opponent and the umpires.

There was an instance in the one-

dayers in Brisbane last summer when he was bowling and a few consecutive lbw shouts didn't go his way, and he was visibly unhappy about it.

But that's the nature of the man – he does tend to blow up.

A couple of season ago he returned to Tasmania so that he could sort his game out before resuming his career. Perhaps the others hadn't tried to practise that method too.

To be fair to Justin Langer, his problems could not be blamed on a lack of commitment. He was the great practiser of the series, and would have been out in the nets having throw-downs from John Buchanan until it was dark almost every night.

Physically exhausted by three days in the field at Calcutta, the bowlers were relieved when Steve Waugh won the toss at Chennai's Chidambaram Stadium and batted on a pitch that all the pundits said would spin. Australia brought in off-spinner Colin Miller for Kasprowicz. India played three frontline spinners, including debutant leggie Bahutule, and Kulkarni. Dighe replaced the injured Mongia behind the stumps.

The opening session was electrifying. Slater left in the first over, loosely edging an angled balled from left-arm quick Zaheer down Laxman's gullet at second slip. Thereafter, Hayden and Langer flayed the combination of pace and spin, racing to 67 in the 12th over, whereupon Langer cut too close to his body and edged to slip ... last man: 35 from 35 balls.

Hayden's footwork destroyed Harbhajan's attack. Down the pitch he drove into the stands over long off and long on, hitting four of the six sixes clouted before

he found himself unwilling to be back in an environment that he'd thought he'd outgrown, and he seemed to be struggling to adjust to the fact.

We heard stories about his sledging of other players. It was as if there was a kind of anger expressing itself because of his circumstances, and this was his release. Again immature, again understandable.

Still, he's a pretty strong-minded character, and I think he's able to get through his disappointments.

Hopefully too he has heard the wiser counsel of the people around him.

Maybe David Boon has had a word to him. One would hope that the senior players can help set younger players straight when they see things go awry.

lunch. And he swept on length, either square or fine, then occasionally over and beyond midwicket.

Following Langer, Mark Waugh prospered and the session ended pulsatingly at 2-140, 100 coming in boundaries. Hayden's aggression and Waugh's deft touches were worth 150, until Waugh was out caught off a miscued drive. Steve Waugh arrived and by the close, he and Hayden had put their team in a virtually unassailable position at 3-326.

The turning point of the Test match came next morning. It involved Steve Waugh, and can only be described as an aberration, one of those extraordinary things that you could only see in cricket, like a flash flood or a car accident when the road seems deserted.

Australia's innings was cruising 40 minutes into the second day. A total of 500-plus seemed comfortably within reach, when Steve Waugh went to sweep a ball from Harbhajan. There was an appeal for lbw as the ball ballooned in the air, bounced and spun towards the

---

Say so... *"Steve Waugh's mistake can only be described as an aberration, one of those extraordinary things that you could only see in the game of cricket, like a flash flood or a car accident when the road seems deserted. "*

---

stumps. Hayden at the non-striker's end yelled, "Look out." Instinctively Waugh, with only one hand on the bat, pushed at the ball with his free right hand.

As soon as he touched it he realised what he had done. For a stunned moment there was no appeal, then Tendulkar led the chorus from extra cover. Umpire Jayaprekash had no choice: Waugh was out, handled ball, becoming only the sixth player in 1535 Tests to be dismissed in this fashion.

What followed was a calamitous collapse. Australia lost 7-65 to be all out for 391 and while it was a solid total, and included a double-century by Hayden, it let

Say so... *on the third day of the Third Test, sensing that the momentum of the match, and with it the series, was drifting away from Australia ...* "*Drop the ego, and stop the boundaries!*" **Greg Matthews**

India back into the game. Once again Harbhajan was the destroyer, with another seven-wicket haul.

India took off from their position of renewed confidence to launch their innings with a century partnership. Das and Ramesh luxuriated on the front foot, emphasising their confidence against full-length new ball bowling, when the ball does not deviate.

Warne and Miller floundered and the partnership reached 123 before Ramesh was dismissed. VVS Laxman, Australia's nemesis, batted with conviction and at stumps the score was 1-211.

Next day, while wickets fell sporadically, Tendulkar made busy with focused application, punishing the under-pitched Australian spin. He raised his 25th Test hundred with a majestic on-drive off Miller for six.

The sense that the momentum of this match, and with it the series, was drifting away from Australia was best expressed by Greg Matthews, who exhorted the Australians from the ABC commentary box to "drop the ego, and stop the boundaries".

The day ended with India at 9-480, and the following morning the home side ended its innings at 501, a lead of 110. There were almost two days left and somehow it felt like a historic shift in the making. The statistics confirmed as much – it was the first time in 124 years of Test cricket that Australia had conceded over 500 runs in the second innings of one Test (657-dec at Calcutta) and the first innings of the next.

If ever there was a time for a team of champions to dig deep, this was it. But at that stage of the tour, Australia's self-belief was perhaps a little undermined. It impacted more on some than others. Ricky Ponting, for instance, had been in pretty ordinary form and the way he'd got out at Calcutta when Australia were trying to save the game just showed what a dreadful mental state he was in. Overall, though, the Australian team remained pretty strong.

However they were up against a team that had in a sense reinvented itself since its second innings at Calcutta. Suddenly the Indians believed in themselves.

When Australia began their second innings, someone in the excitable Tamil crowd flung up a sign; "Can we bang the Kangaroos again?" Hayden and Slater gave an emphatic answer and did most of the banging, adding 82, before Hayden was out for 35.

He'd had a great series, contributed 549 runs at a Bradmanesque average of 109.8, all the more remarkable since he had no reputation against spin.

But once again, Harbhajan Singh was magnificent. Over after over he just kept landing the ball superbly. I think he surprised his own supporters as much as the Australians. Hayden got after him and got on top of him ... but Harbhajan came back.

To do so showed extraordinary maturity and

Say so... *"Harbhajan Singh was magnificent. Over after over he just kept landing the ball superbly, surprising his own supporters as much as the Australians. Hayden got after him and got on top of him ... but Harbhajan came back."*

---

strength of character, qualities in such a young man that invited speculation in the commentary box. Maybe his background was a factor – he's a Sikh from Punjab and they're regarded as mentally tough people. His father had died recently, further testing his determination to continue and succeed.

He had overcome other setbacks, having played against Australia back in 1998 when there had been a question mark about his action. He had passed scrutiny with the committee at the ICC only after modifying his style of delivery. Also he'd been at India's cricket academy and had been thrown out for alleged bad

Say so...

"If anyone in the Australian contingent had happened to be superstitious, this would have been a good time to polish up the good luck charms. A similar thought had apparently already occurred to Mr Subramanian."

behaviour, so there was a streak of rebelliousness in him. As someone like Shane Warne might attest, that can be a good thing. It's all very well to have a good team ethic and play for a cause, but you don't want to stamp out a player's individuality.

With Hayden gone, Harbhajan proved his worth yet again against Gilchrist. In a bid for quick runs, the wicket-keeper was promoted to first drop but failed to read Harbhajan's arm ball, no doubt to the delight of another fan who placarded "I didn't bring lunch today because Harbhajan promised me some wickets."

Slater soon followed, and then the Waughs resisted superbly, grinding out a modest lead. Harbhajan's awkward bounce was always threatening, and wickets continued to fall. Shane Warne was lbw to the last ball of the day. At 7-241 Australia had a moderate advantage of 131.

At breakfast next morning, the final day of the match, Jason Gillespie was asked how many was enough to win. Ever the optimist, he said 160, not a bad guess. In just over an hour of anxious batting Australia squeezed out another 23 runs.

Harbhajan bedevilled them, bagging eight innings wickets, 15 for the match, totalling 32 for the series.

So much for Kumble's absence. India were left needing 155 to win from 70 overs.

If anyone in the Australian contingent had happened to be superstitious, this would have been a good time to polish up the good luck charms. A similar thought had apparently already occurred to Mr Subramanian.

As I mentioned earlier, from the moment that my

sandalwood statue of Ganesha, the Hindu elephant god, arrived in the commentary box the fortunes changed for our technical problems – and for India. We seemed to have removed all the obstacles on both fronts.

On the last morning at Chennai, Mr Subramanian arrived in the box carrying his shapeless old airways bag. Serious as ever, he unzipped it and out came an assortment of exotica. Two incense sticks went up in front of Mr Ganesha, which Mr Subramanian lit – a heady element in the enclosed box. Next came flowers, hibiscus and rose petals. He also produced fruit, an orange or two, a tangerine, and then some channa, a savoury chickpea delicacy in a little bowl.

All this was arranged around the Ganesha, along with a coconut-flavoured sweet, and other homemade delicacies to which we were invited to help ourselves. This was Mr Subramanian's puja ceremony, his prayers,

Acts of Waugh

AUSTRALIA'S CAPTAIN IS NOT GIVEN TO ROMANTICISE ABOUT ANYTHING. AND HE PLAYS A TOUGH GAME.

Lindsay Hassett said a long while ago, you only notice captains when they're losing. I wonder if he'd revise his opinion if he were around today, or if he'd feel the laid-back style of Steve Waugh proves the point yet again.

Allan Border, Mark Taylor and Steve Waugh have shared the gift of a great cricket brain. To borrow from my early training as a commentator, it's about anticipation once again.

It's also about having the courage of your convictions, to see that this is the time to bowl this bloke, this is the time to put the fieldsman there ... and to *do* it.

It takes guts, and it takes experience. Steve Waugh was reluctant to follow his gut instinct early on in his captaincy. In the West Indies in '99 when things were running against Australia, he wasn't too sure. It's a different story nowadays.

He's very approachable, in my experience of him, with pretty solid views about cricket and life. He's not given to romanticise about anything, in fact he can be fairly blunt.

There's no doubt, too, that he plays a tough game. He's combative in the tradition that goes back to Ian Chappell. There's a ruthlessness about Waugh that which we soon discovered were not just in aid of the commentary box but also had an ulterior motive. As he went about his devotions, with ash across his forehead and his little dot between his eyes, someone outside the box started taking photos.

Mr Subramanian had lined up a Reuters photographer to cover this prayer meeting. He laughed it off, but beneath the surface lurked a shrewd mind. The following day he would be interviewed on Indian television about how he came to be in the Australian radio box. The first episode of his life story perhaps, and a further step in Mr Subramanian's media career?

Australian captain Steve Waugh. How far would he go to win?

India started its pursuit of 155 for victory about 45 minutes prior to lunch, with a minimum of 70 overs to be bowled in the day. One way or another, a result was going to be posted. However, yet another reminder may also be more to do with the influence of Bradman on Australian cricket.

How far would he go in order to win?

When I put it to him that in allowing Michael Slater to misbehave on the field in the First Test in India he had ducked his reponsibility, Waugh was dismissive.

"You can't be a schoolmaster all the time," he said.

In my book that is ducking it. And not just in my book — it's written in the laws that a captain's job on the field is to keep charge of his players.

Why did it happen? I think it's because somewhere inside Steve Waugh, and not too far from the surface, is a man who likes to take it to the opposition in every way he can. Of course he wouldn't go over the top, but he has talked about "mental disintegration", his euphemism for sledging. And what else is sledging but a kind of gamesmanship, a way of getting some pyschological advantage over the opponent?

It's pretty clear these tactics have been around for a long time in Australia. If you're standing at silly point and the batsman has been a bit out of form and you offer some remark that may not be directed directly at him but around him, it's got to have some effect.

Perhaps it has always been part of the game. Whether it's more prevalent now than it used to be is a question. Whether it gets a bit out of hand, too.

How much does Steve condone it, or do it himself?

The answer to that may have to do with the Eleventh Commandment — thou shalt not be caught.

that we were in India, it would not be without its moments of unexpected humour.

After McGrath sent down the first over of the innings there was a farcical delay of 15 minutes – the sightscreen attendants at the far end couldn't get the screen to close, leaving a large advertising logo with a red background, exposed to the batsman.

There was frantic activity as ground staff came running from everywhere, including straight across the middle of the ground. White sheets were called for and they attempted to drape them over the advertising sign. Some of the Australians even wandered off the ground. Eventually, two ground staff, who were perched up high on the screen, found that repeated kicking of the offending area had an affect. The screen eventually slid back over the logo and play resumed.

Shortly before lunch India lost Das on a miscued lobbed catch to McGrath. Then Laxman took charge, flinging boundaries off the spinners. Warne again took a mauling. Ramesh's run out at 2-76 broke the flow, and once more Gillespie bent his back tellingly, removing Tendulkar and Ganguly via the sure hands of Mark

Say so... *"McGrath returned, and Mark Waugh held a catch: eight wickets down. For Australia, though, it was too much to hope for. The impossible remained just that. Soon afterwards Harbhajan struck the winning runs."*

Waugh in the slips. Dravid's loose drive to Steve Waugh at mid-off hinted at panic. At tea they were 5-132.

It was do or die. India had five wickets in hand and needed only 23 runs in the final session to claim the Test and the series.

Bold to the last, Waugh persisted with Miller. It paid off – in his first over after the break he had Laxman caught by Mark Waugh, who dived at mid-wicket to complete a brilliant two-handed catch.

Things got worse for India when Bahutule edged Miller to Warne at first slip in the same over to depart without scoring. At 7-135, the improbable suddenly

looked possible. The hosts had lost 5/34 and the
Australians sniffed victory.

As Dighe picked off a few telling fours, McGrath
returned, and Mark Waugh thrillingly held his sixth
catch: a nervous 8-151.

For Australia, though, it was too much to hope for.
The impossible remained just that.

The harbinger of India's success, Harbhajan Singh
drove his first two deliveries from McGrath hard to
Steve Waugh at extra cover. He then pushed McGrath
towards midwicket where Langer gathered and threw at
the non-striker's stumps. The ball flew high. Had it hit,
Harbhajan would have been run out without scoring.

Soon afterwards Harbhajan rapturously, and
fittingly, struck the winning runs off McGrath. At the
start of the over India required two runs for victory.
The first delivery was full and wide of off-stump, to

Lessons to Learn

It was the batting that really cost
Australia the series. While Hayden
was a revelation with his 549 runs at
109.8, the next best was Steve Waugh
with 243 at 48.6. After that, things
looked pretty bleak.

Langer's lowest score was 19, but
he failed to convert any of his starts
into a large score, finishing with 161
runs at 32.2. Slater never reached 50,
making his 166 runs at an average of
33.2. Mark Waugh came good in the
last Test with two half-centuries, but
his return for the series was a mere
149 runs at 29.8.

The two biggest disappointments
were Ponting and Gilchrist. Ponting's
17 runs in five innings included three
ducks. He fell to Harbhajan in each
innings he played.

Gilchrist made a magnificent 122 in
the First Test at Mumbai, and I think
he got carried away by his attacking
method. In the various innings that
came after that he just didn't give
himself a chance to get in.

It was as if he were swept away.
He scored just two more runs in his
next four innings, including a king pair
in Calcutta.

Collectively, the batsmen had three
series-turning sessions in which seven
wickets fell – the second session on
the opening day at Calcutta and the
final session of the same Test, where
they should have held on for a draw,
and then the opening session on
the second day at Chennai, after
they resumed at 3-326, only to be
bowled out for 391.

which Harbhajan offered an open blade. The ball flew along the ground through point. The batsmen completed two and the crowd of 45,000 erupted.

For a moment or two, the players stood still in the middle, as if they wanted confirmation that that scoreboard was correct.

Then the realisation sank in for everyone. The Indian players streamed on to the ground.

Australia had been glorious in their narrow defeat. Defeat nonetheless, and the dream of winning in India for the first time since 1969 was destroyed.

For India it had been one of the greatest comebacks in Test history. They were only the seventh team to win a three-Test series after losing the opening Test match.

But surely, no other team had ever come back from having followed-on in the second Test some 270-odd runs in arrears. For Australia, it was, quite literally, the one that got away.

Harbhajan and Hayden were named jointly

Say so... *"I don't think we did anything wrong. India just picked themselves up very well. They showed that they are a tough side. They fought back well. It's Test match cricket."* **Steve Waugh**

as men of a series that hopefully revived the passion for Test cricket in India.

I think the Australian players enjoyed the series. Obviously they were disappointed to lose, because they thought after the First Test and two days of the Second Test they were going to win in a canter.

And if there's any truth in the line that it was good for the game, then, yes, I don't think there's any doubt about that. It may just sharpen our fellows up.

I don't think there's any doubt that we'll be back in India more often than ever. We've been in 1998 and 2001, and with Tendulkar such a huge personality in the game – among others, such as Laxman and Harbhajan – I'm sure we're going to be back soon.

My lasting impressions were still vivid a month or two later when I wrote in the "ABC Cricket Book":

"Cricket's enchantment persists. Memories of the contests at Eden Gardens and the Chidambaram Stadium linger happily, excitingly, beyond the statistical postscript of another inconsequential one-day series.

"The roaring, pulsating crowds who saw Laxman's powerful, flawless strokes, and those who risked heart failure watching their heroes falter, panic and somehow scramble to victory, have enjoyed the ultimate sporting experience.

"Character, quality, aberration, unpredictability, injustice, bravery, misjudgment and thrilling desperation created unforgettable drama.

"Is it too much to hope that the Ashes series can produce matches of comparable excitement? The expectation is enough to keep screens glowing and radios burbling throughout antipodean nights."

My last sight of Mr Subramanian was after the game at Chennai. One of the things he always liked to do at the end of the day was carry *my* bags, and only mine in particular, down to the car. He seemed to think it was part of his role, though to me it was a peculiarly subservient thing to do.

On this last occasion, however, Mr Subramanian came and joined a few of us at the cricket club at the ground. Peter Roebuck was staying there – it's a lovely club with gymnasium, squash courts, the works – and he was in a very lively mood, holding court on many matters, most notably the Indian captaincy and the bribery scandal, and buying beers all over the place. We had a great old chinwag down there.

I hope we parted on happy terms with Mr Subramanian, but there was some dispute at the end about payment. We'd been paying him a certain amount for each game, plus train fares, but in Calcutta,

At the start of the series, as Bishan Bedi had gloomily observed, India were without Anil Kumble, their only spinner of worth. How the world can change in four short weeks. Harbhajan Singh's match figures in the Third Test were 15/217. Only Narendra Hirwani's 16/136 on debut against the West Indies, on the same ground in 1987/88, prevented Harbhajan from registering the best-ever Test match figures by an Indian. In consecutive Test matches he had claimed hauls of 13 and 15 wickets. It was the best two-Test performance since Jim Laker's 11- and 19-wicket efforts against Australia in 1956. His tally of 32 wickets at an average of 17.03, was a staggering 29 better than his nearest team-mates, Tendulkar and Zaheer. He captured 64 per cent of his team's wickets in the series. At just 20 years of age he had a huge future ahead of him. Who now was talking about Anil Kumble?

because his relative no longer lived there, he had had to stay in a hotel, and ever since he'd been at us for reimbursement. Now, we certainly didn't dismiss this out of hand – Glenn Mitchell and I talked it over a number of times, and we even asked Harsha Bhogle for his opinion – but in the end we felt that as we were paying him well over the odds for his daily fee, we'd done enough. Rather bluntly we drew the line.

Whether or not Mr Subramanian took this in good part, or whether he went off in a huff, I don't know.

I'm sure if we were to invite him to Australia for the next series he'd jump at the opportunity.

But then again, I don't think we could afford the train fares from India...

After the drama of the mentally-draining Third Test match, a week off would have been perfect. Instead, just three days later, a group of exhausted players moved from Chennai to Bangalore to start the series of five one-day matches.

There were casualties even before play began. Jason Gillespie, who'd survived three matches without any recurrence of back problems, was immediately sent home on suspicion of breakdown.

Australia's resilience and the continuation of Matthew Hayden's remarkable batting form were the main reasons for the final 3-2 winning margin achieved by Steve Waugh's team. Highlights included:

• For India Tendulkar became the first player to pass 10,000 international one-day runs with a typically savage innings of 139 at Indore. Laxman maintained his excellent form from the Calcutta epic, and the left-handed Badani batted impressively in Pune.

• In Bangalore, in a blazing start, India passed 100 in the 15th over, and were all out in the last over for an imposing 315, with a starring century from Shewag. Australia chased solidly until Bevan's departure to a sharp Robin Singh catch, and Hayden, who'd been belatedly added to the squad after his outstanding Test

Say so... "*Our mantra has been: don't have bad sessions, because that loses Test matches. But in this series we had three really bad sessions and it cost us two Test matches.*" **Steve Waugh**

series, was nailed lbw by Shewag on 99. The momentum faded, and India's win halted Australia's winning one-day sequence at 10. Alas for Shewag, he fractured a finger and did not play again in the series.

• In Pune Australia easily ran down India's 9-248 with five overs in hand. Mark Waugh scored his 18th one-day century. Ganguly, who again failed with the bat, clearly dissented the umpire's decision when a mix-up resulted in the run out of Darren Lehmann. Ganguly gestured angrily, believing the batsmen had not crossed, and therefore Steve Waugh should have been given out. Match referee Cammie Smith, who had fined Gilchrist and McGrath for dissent in Bangalore, took no action.

• At Indore Tendulkar pulverised the Australian bowling with his 28th one-day hundred; 139 from 125 balls. Australia, who'd rested Matthew Hayden and were missing Mark Waugh with a fractured finger, succumbed by 118 runs.

• At the east coastal fishing city of Vishakhapatnam, Hayden's maiden one-day hundred in a revelling 219 run partnership with Ponting, who rediscovered form, led to a match-winning 4-338. Australia won by 93 runs to square the series.

• In the decider at the ubiquitous Nehru Stadium, this one in Fatorda, near Goa, Ganguly celebrated his early arrival at the toss by winning it, and making runs: 74 from 83 balls, while Laxman serenely moved to his maiden one-day century. Chasing 6-266, Gilchrist rampaged to 50 from 28 balls. A middle-order slump did not include Bevan's vital wicket, and from 6-202 in the 40th over, Harvey struck robustly to help Bevan finish off the task with two overs to spare.

Hayden's Indian summer continued, claiming another Man-of-the-Series award.

England

Only the most optimistic England
supporter could see a home win in
the Ashes series. Having lost in India,
the champion Australians arrived in
a fighting frame of mind.

In February I received a note from John
Woodcock, the distinguished English cricket
correspondent, saying how fortunate I was to be
going to India, because he believed that series would
provide the best cricket of the year.

The inference was that England were unlikely to
stretch Australia as much as India in a home contest,
and events subsequently vindicated John's assessment.

Like Liston versus Clay, it's easy to talk up
the prospect of a big showdown, but in the case of
the Ashes battle only the most optimistic England
camp follower could see a home win, and most
balanced observers were hoping the result would
be no worse than 3-1.

For my part the tour offered a rare chance to
describe some matches in England, an undertaking
that I had experienced only once before on radio, in
the 1983 World Cup.

In the sense that broadcasting is a privilege and not
a right, I was delighted at last to have such an
opportunity – I'll avoid the temptation here to go
into chapter and verse about the reasons for this
opportunity failing to materialise before.

Suffice to say that Tim Lane, my respected
colleague, and arguably the finest all-round sports
commentator of the day, and myself, had been available
in the past but didn't get selected.

For 2001 we would be splitting the tour, which
meant that I would be covering the one-dayers and the
First Test, and Tim would do the remaining four Tests.

I had been to England many times, mainly as a
tourist or touring cricketer, and to finally get the chance
to follow at least part of an Ashes campaign was a
tremendous thrill, and an experience to savour working
with the most celebrated cricket broadcasting team in
the world — TMS: the BBC's Test Match Special team.

The relaxed atmosphere in the box had been created
during Brian Johnston's era of leg-pulls and frivolity,
and although no one could possibly emulate him, his
spirit lived on with Jonathan Agnew and Henry Blofeld.
They always saw the lighter side, and recognised that

Jeff Thomson was a welcome
guest in the commentary box; he
is seen here with veteran BBC
expert Henry "Blowers" Blofeld.
Thommo was involved in the TV
broadcasts too, the late-night
timing of which in Australia
generated a fair amount of heat.

cricket was basically just a game; to be respected of course, but not revered like Christians in high church, or peers in the House of Lords.

The value-added dimension of my tour was a toy called a digital camera. The camera, as one of my snapper colleagues, David Gray, would describe it, was idiot proof. Aim, hit the trigger, save or discard, and then download into my laptop and fire off the pictures as an attachment to an email.

This toy gave the excuse, not that I needed it, to roam the country, and brighten up the look of the cricket section of the ABC website.

The snap of a mallard, a magnificently coloured, breast-pumping, feather-farmed duck, taken above a stream at Bourton-on-the-Water in the Cotswolds, was a highlight, and attracted over 260,000 hits in one day on the ABC site.

Between ducks and diversions to Castle Howard, the Woburn Safari Park and the national racing museum at Newmarket, I saw a few one-day matches, and managed to capture a snap of a cricket ball floating in the River Chelm, after Brett Lee had launched the

Say so... *on being cleared of any wrongdoing in the betting scandal...* "*I'm very pleased. It has been a long road. It was difficult but I just tried to blot it out and play cricket to the best of my ability.*" **Mark Waugh**

ball out of the ground at Chelmsford against Essex.

Lee's early return from injury at Cardiff in the opening one-day game took everyone by surprise, as he wasn't expected to play until the Ashes section of the tour. He was quick, underdone, and wayward enough to have 85 struck from 10 overs. Pakistan made only 257, and Australia won stylishly on Ponting's run-a-ball 70, with enough overs and wickets in hand to suggest top form was imminent.

England had a show in the match at Bristol, Trescothick's 69 a hint of his ability, and in a tight chase the Aussie Gloucester man, Ian Harvey, whacked

Steeped in History

....

THE APPEAL OF CRICKET IN ENGLAND IS BEGUILING.

How can I describe the appeal of cricket in England? There's an aroma about the game, it's just steeped in history, like going into a cathedral.

I look forward to the lovely, soft light, so different from the harsh light in Australia. There's a sort of relaxed smell to the game, particularly on those older English grounds — the texture and feel are appetising, though certainly not the food, which does often leave something to be desired. The beer's not too bad, but, oh, those cold pies and the stodge. I miss our fresh fruit and salads.

I've made good friends in England through cricket. Peter Roebuck's name comes to mind. There's Ian Davies, a great Northampton supporter and former sports correspondent for the BBC World Service — I've stayed with him a few times. And I've got to know commentator Christopher Martin-Jenkins over the years.

My memories of England go back to '72 when I was there with the Australian Old Collegians, and in '75, '78 and later on in '89 with the Old Cranbrookians.

It was magnificent playing on the lovely old grounds, at Arundel, at Tunbridge Wells, at Sevenoaks, there were so many of them. The one I remember best was at Swansea, where the boundaries were so short I hit a six off a thick inside edge. Maybe that's why I like those English grounds — small boundaries.

And there are the other nice experiences, too, going out with your friends, the village green atmosphere, the pub over the road, the long lunch out the front just watching the game.

> "THE VILLAGE GREEN ATMOSPHERE ... THE PUB OVER THE ROAD ... THE LONG LUNCH WATCHING THE GAME ..."

All the pleasantries of an English summer.

Over the weeks I spent reporting on the tour, my little Peugeot 306 darted over 5000km all over England, and not just to the cricket matches. For an Australian, with the sun on your back and the thermometer touching 30 degrees, believe it or not, I thought once again that it is the most beautiful place in the world.

The conditions are just perfect for lying back and enjoying the game.

Our welcome was as warm as always. Many, many people stressed how they loved seeing the way the Australians play and carry themselves — aggressive yet stylish, with dignity yet always refreshingly full of vitality. The Aussie team were a lot of fun to be with, and of course they had every reason to smile.

Picture Story

....

MY NEW CAMERA WENT WITH ME EVERYWHERE.

Away from the cricket I took a diversion and dived into the countryside, just to take in some of the delights of village life. The sun was streaming down and, following the exceptionally wet English winter, the countryside was looking magnificent.

My biggest problem was when I got on those M roads, the freeways — the drivers moved quickly and no one seemed to be much concerned about the 70mph (110km/h) speed limit. I got caught up in a flying cortege one day, going about 90mph (150km/h), and a police car just zipped past on the right. They must have had somewhere else to go

Get on the back roads, Jim, and calm down.

Some of my digitised snapshots — opposite page, clockwise from top left: The idyllic setting at Arundel, and the spectators there; ball in the water, courtesy Brett Lee; village scene; World War II fighter aeroplane at historic aviation museum; Henry VIII's palace at Hampton Court; English weather; working at Arundel.

This page, clockwise from below left: Presentation time at Lord's; Steve gives his views; bets are on at Nottingham for the one-dayers; stand-up turn at the same venue.

a superb six over the cover boundary in the penultimate over to finish off the good work done again by Ponting with a century.

In their first day/night match in England, played at Old Trafford, the Australians took full advantage of a change in the conditions, which made the staging of day/night cricket in England look ridiculous. The rain freshened the pitch, and the bowling of Gillespie was unplayable, with the ball gripping and moving around impossibly. The team batting first in these television extravaganzas, had a significant advantage, which made the toss as loaded as knowing which chamber held the bullet in Russian roulette.

At Trent Bridge against Pakistan, when both teams had already qualified for the Final, Australia had their first experience of the new security measures, designed to prevent pitch invasions, or at least delay them until the players were off the field.

A line of plastic hessian, about the height of a picket fence was to be held up at the raiding hour, a tactic that apparently had worked well when tried at a rugby match at Twickenham. The punditry advised that there

Say so... "*I'm very keen. I'm 32 and it could be my last tour of England, I don't know yet. All I want to do is take some catches, make some runs and get some poles (wickets). That's all.*" **Shane Warne**

weren't many Pakistani rugby fans, and like a thief who wants to break into a house, the invaders usually find a way of reaching their target.

Throughout the one-day series the police had adopted a kid-glove approach to the problem, for fear, it seemed, of being discriminatory.

Common sense suggested that if there was a potential problem, move in and sort it out, even if the outcome was eviction from the ground.

Allowing the supporters of the Pakistani team to bring in flags and horns, and firecrackers as well, was asking for trouble, and the security system was somewhere between archaic, anarchic and non-existent.

On the field Australia were unbeatable, when it mattered. They inflicted further psychological damage on England at the Oval in a "net" before the Final, bowling them out for 176 and winning with 20 overs and eight wickets in hand.

And at Lord's they repeated their World Cup win over Pakistan, who were intimidated by Australia's confident, composed aggression, succumbing for 152. Gilchrist's splendid batting made for a nine-wicket margin, and 23 overs to spare.

The beer can that hit Michael Bevan at the match presentation was the only grievous blow Australia sustained in the tournament. No joke, of course, and the incident soured Australia's galumphing success. It may also be the last public appearance by a team at the conclusion of a one-day series in England. As Lord's is run by the MCC, I doubt that their members will give up the right to bring wine bottles and beer cans into the ground in future. What's good for the members, is OK for the rest. No wonder they have security problems.

Australia's zestful, exciting cricket attacked and overwhelmed the opposition. Injuries to Nasser Hussain and Graham Thorpe certainly weakened England's effort, a factor that repeated in the Test series. But could they have withstood the high quality of the Australian bowling and catching? Try it on the computer, and you might get a contest. Whoever said a good game is a fast game, must have been watching Steve Waugh's team.

❅

It's an impossible decision to say who is the best Australian cricketer I've seen.

I remember O'Neill and Harvey as being wonderful players. Other outstanding memories: Alan Davidson's ability to move the ball; Benaud's imaginative captaincy and his positive approach; Bob Simpson's tremendous gifts as a player – probably the finest slip fielder we'd ever seen, until Mark Waugh and Mark Taylor came on the scene.

Jeff Thomson want down very well in the BBC commentary box while we were doing the coverage. There's still something of the scallywag about him that appeals to the English – even though he's very much the silver-haired fast bowler these days. He was part of the television commentary team too, but I don't think there's any doubt that we got far more value out of him on radio. It's the nature of the medium. We got more of his candid, refreshing humour – very much to the point, self-deprecatory too.

He loved responding to jibes from Jonathan Agnew about the Poms and the Aussies – and they loved having him in the box.

Graham McKenzie was a wonderful bowler who did it all on his own. Then there was Lillee, an outstanding fast bowler who changed from an out-and-out quick to a very cunning fast-medium swing-and-cut bowler after his back injury. He was a magnificent bowler but McGrath's even better. He has taken it to another level because of his relentlessness.

And then there's Shane Warne who has probably done more for the image of wrist-spin bowling than anyone in memory.

And then there's the Chappells... the list goes on.

What, then, of the best I've seen of England?

There have been a lot of good players, but no great ones, in my years of watching it.

I never saw Jack Hobbs or WG Grace – they must have been remarkable – or Walter Hammond. Botham was a wonderful all-round player and in the 1981 series he really excited everybody. But he couldn't maintain that across the board. His record against the West Indies, for a player of his stature, is poor. There has been Ted Dexter, and Cowdrey, and Ken Barrington was as good an English batsman as I've ever seen. Geoff

Say so... *on his shared 36th birthday with twin brother Mark while on tour...* **"***The girls normally buy our presents. I've let him open the innings and if he's lucky he might get a bowl. Or unlucky.***"** **Steve Waugh**

Boycott couldn't be faulted for technical perfection, allowing for the fact that he wasn't a team player, and I used to admire John Edrich and David Gower.

But of all the players I've seen over the last 20 years, Graham Gooch stands out as the best English cricketer. And yet, he had his weaknesses, he was fallible against well-organised bowling and tactics.

And this begs the question: what's wrong with English cricket today?

It's partly a state of mind, partly that they haven't got a hard enough internal cricket competition in the county championship.

What the Eye Doesn't See...

....

SO WHAT DO THOSE PLAYERS REALLY GET UP TO?

I'm sometimes asked about the "real" story of what players get up to behind the scenes. My answer is that they relax, sure, and there's still a bit of the macho tradition of the sport – that thing about getting out and having a few drinks and a good time.

There were some in the past who perhaps did lose control. On tour players sometimes did things that people turned a blind eye to. A fair bit was allowed to go through to the keeper, as the saying goes.

However the degree of expectation that's laid on today's Australian players is enormous. The level of performance in everything they do is under examination. In the main, they don't have time to get up to what players of earlier eras used to be able to do. They don't have the down time.

> "THE DEGREE OF EXPECTATION ON PLAYERS IS ENORMOUS. MISBEHAVE? IT'S A WONDER THEY FIND THE TIME TO."

In addition they have problems with the continual invasion of their privacy.

Fans are always in the foyers, always in their faces, always asking for autographs, always looking for photos to be taken with them.

As if all that weren't enough, today's players have to handle the ever-increasing emphasis on the team ethos, the counselling sessions, the meetings, the games they play together on tour to keep themselves motivated. Misbehaviour? It's a wonder any of them find the time to misbehave.

Still, everyone's human, as they say. Things do happen. And though there's less validity in the one-time mantra "what plays on tour stays on tour", it's still up to the players to take care of themselves. Away from the cricket, when you're in the public eye, obviously you've got to be wary. It comes with the territory. If you were a lesser light then no one would know.

In the past, as long as players treated people fairly, they could afford to go out and have a good time, maybe even cross someone's bows occasionally, and it wouldn't matter much. Nowadays I think they're all pretty wary. Particularly on an Ashes tour there's always the risk of somebody trying to line them up.

There's a suspicion of the English tabloids for obvious reasons, as Shane Warne has found out to his cost more than once. Michael Slater and Ricky Ponting have had their moments too. You don't have to be royalty or a pop star to get set up.

But it's a combination of other things too.

Does cricket mean as much in England as it used to? From what I hear there's not enough being played in the schools. Soccer is the game they're all playing and its tribalism has taken over.

Cricket always seems a sport that should have been invented and developed in Australia, not England. It's a classic example of a country picking up a game that someone else invented, and running with it a lot harder and with more determination than the originators.

The history of Anglo-Australian cricket proves the point. When the Australians are keen and they've got a bit of talent, they win. England have had periods of success but not a lot for a long while.

You could make generalisations about the desire to win, and even about the attitude in England to everything in life. Maybe in defence of England you could say that it's a more sophisticated society, where people who have a scintilla of intelligence

Excuse me, Mr Packer...

MOGUL KERRY PACKER AND TELEVISION CRICKET ARE SYNONYMOUS. SO IT'S A BRAVE — OR FOOLISH — MAN WHO HAS THE TEMERITY TO QUESTION HIS METHODS.

What are the television channels doing with their rights to the cricket, and where can the poor viewing consumer go when he/she isn't properly served?

Channel Seven's attitude towards the cricket during the Ashes tour is an example of the problem.

The Ashes are supposed to be a "listed" event, available on free-to-air television, but despite widespread criticism, Channel Seven, like Nine before them, refused to put the matches on until 10 or 11 at night.

And they got away with it. It's crazy.

They shouldn't be allowed to do it. It's an example of the greed that overtakes people who run big organisations.

They buy up the rights, and then they relegate the whole thing to late at night. They lock advertisers into whatever banal repeats they choose to run and they'd rather go with that than the cricket. If you buy something, why not deliver on it?

The whole reason Kerry Packer got involved in cricket in the first place, particularly in Australia, was because of the ratings and the requirement for Australian content. When he saw the decide to use it elsewhere than on the sportsfield.

My colleague in the commentary box Peter Roebuck knows both ends of the argument from personal experience, and it's something he has often spoken about. It might be harsh, but I can hear his words: "In Australia there is always the sense of people striving for something. In England you don't feel that."

In cricket, it's easy to generalise, but our so-called lucky country always seems to me to have been a place where people strive to get ahead, to do something. They grasp the opportunities.

And we've got a wonderful climate – that's as strong a reason as any for our doing so well in sport. We don't have those awful European winters when you spend most of your life indoors.

following the ABC got in 1972 when they did the last session of the last day of the Fifth Test at the Oval, that's what triggered his brainwave.

Bingo – there's audience in cricket!

As recently as March 2001, when the India tour was not on free-to-air television, the radio audience for the ABC coverage was enormous. Our ratings at the time went through the roof.

Of course there may be other factors at work too. People are rusted on to ABC Radio like they're rusted on to TV. People who listen to ABC Radio don't like ads, and I must admit I share that view.

Driving around I sometimes hit the car radio buttons, and what do I get … an ad! So I go back somewhere else and get … another ad!. People like me can't cop that

kind of radio. I'm a typical ABC listener. If the interview isn't particularly interesting on Radio National or BL I go to FM and listen to some music.

And I can't put up with the demagoguery on some commercial radio. It would drive you lunatic.

This problem of television coverage isn't new, of course, in fact it was the cause of a memorable spat between me and Kerry Packer. And he's a man you don't offend if you value a quiet life.

I started doing international cricket commentary in the year that World Series Cricket hit the headlines.

I still remember being in Packer's office on the day in 1977 when the official announcement was made. It was a press conference, and there were Packer and his team, and a bevy of reporters.

Packer had a bank of cigarettes in front of him, like the backload of a semi-trailer strewn across the desk, and he was drawing them out one after another. I've never seen anything like the way he was sucking on those things.

We sat there dutifully while he launched into his spiel about what WSC was all about, all the great players they had signed up, and what a great show it was going to be. On and on it went.

When it came time for questions, Jim Bonner, a provocative current affairs reporter from the ABC, saw a chance that was too good to miss.

"Some people have likened World Series Cricket to World Championship Wrestling," he said. "What would you say to that, Mr Packer?"

It was as if Vesuvius had erupted. The water that had been simmering all of a sudden boiled. You could see the steam coming out of the man's ears.

"World Championship Wrestling," he exploded, "is a joke. It has always been a joke! It continues to be a joke! We are talking about some of the greatest players in the history of the game ..."

Jim had done his business. He'd loaded it up, he'd hit the button, and he'd got the response. And when you're a reporter and that happens, you sit there and say, right, baby, take me away. Keep getting riled, that's what we want to hear.

I've had a few dealings with Kerry Packer over the years. He played cricket with the Old Cranbrookians Cricket Club occasionally, back in the late 1960s when Frank Packer, his father, was still running the family business. I can still remember Kerry down at the ground one day catching

sight of a Triumph TR6 sports car that belonged to one of the other players.

It was a pretty impressive car for its day, and Kerry was interested briefly.

"Mind if I have a spin?" he said to the owner. In he jumped, roared around and brought it back.

"Yeah," he said, "it's not bad, it's got a bit of toe." It was just a plaything to him.

Our paths continued to cross from time, but it was many years later that we had our one and only real confrontation. A very public one it was, too. The setting was yet another press conference, around 1993 by now, when Channel Nine announced with the Australian Cricket Board that they'd signed up another 10 years on their rights agreement.

They had called the conference at Sydney's Wentworth Hotel – Bruce Gyngell, James Packer and all the heavies from Channel Nine were there – but as a news story it was a non-event.

At the time Australia were playing in South Africa and Channel Nine had the rights to telecast, but they were only putting it on late at night, either live or in replay. They weren't doing matches live in actual time.

In contrast, ABC Radio was covering the tour live and rating very well. As far as we were concerned it was terrific that Channel Nine chose not to use its rights fully. From the ABC's point of view, only a fool would stick his hand up and draw attention to the fact – a fool like me.

There were no questions from the floor at first, so I put one to Graham Halbish, the chief executive of the ACB.

"Is the ACB concerned about the lack of live coverage of cricket from South Africa on television?"

Halbish started to give the party line about the ACB's lack of control over the rights outside Australia, and so on,

Packer's steam pressure gauge, however, was on the rise, just like all those years earlier. I could see his movement, that big, dangerous presence on the edge of the field. He interrupted.

"Wait a moment, wait a moment," he said. "Can I respond to this?"

intimidating person when he's like that. The press boys were writing all this stuff down as he continued to rant and glower and get redder and more irate.

I had my tape recorder on, and though the sound quality was far from ideal, I did get a faithful enough representation of what he said to use in a report that night.

I'll always remember the end of the conference. As he left, he strode down the

As he left the conference, he stopped when he reached me. He loomed over me, looking predatory. "Are you from the ABC?" he said.

And he got up and came over to the microphone. The press boys, who'd been waiting for something to write about, were ready. Bang!

"We *are* covering it," he said.

I looked around, and everyone was looking at me.

"But, Mr Packer," I said, "the other night you ran that movie of Clint Eastwood's, 'Dirty Harry', for about the fourth time. The cricket was live from South Africa but you didn't put it on till 11 o'clock at night. I mean, you might be running it, but it's not live."

He glared at me. And he said, "You obviously have no understanding of the Broadcasting Act. Don't you understand that it is our duty to acknowledge that there are other tastes in the audience, not just people who want to watch cricket? We are required under the legislation to provide comprehensive coverage ..."

Off he went on this tangent.

"But, Mr Packer," I persisted, "you've got the cricket. It's not live."

He was furious. He's a seriously

aisle but stopped when he reached me. He loomed over me, looking predatory.

"Are you from the ABC?" he said.

I've often thought what I'd say if I had my time over again.

I wonder how "Are you from Channel Nine?" would have gone down.

Issues of rights and coverage apart, I think that Channel Nine has done a wonderful job with cricket. Technically speaking, its coverage is light years ahead of what anyone else has tried to do, with the possible exception of Channel Four in England in recent times.

Packer's personal influence has been enormous and it has been for the good of the game. At Channel Nine there was always a real hunger and enthusiasm to do the very best they could.

They're not perfect of course, who is? The commercials are a problem in Test matches, but they've tried to get around that by recording what happens between overs and dropping it in later. With the one-day games it doesn't matter as much, every over is a package within the package.

Here you can spend your whole life outside and that creates a sense of freedom and enterprise. It's kind of imbued, that combination of forces – our climate, our sporting tradition, our heroes, and the kids who want to emulate them.

And the combativeness and aggression are a very important part of why the Aussies are successful. When Steve Waugh's team are rolling they seriously intimidate their opponents.

The other teams are catching up. The South

Say so... *on making a duck, and losing, against Australia in the match at Old Trafford...* "*This good run we've had in Test cricket — the real test is when we play the best side in the world.*" **Alec Stewart**

Africans have always had a mental toughness – there is a tradition there too – though I think we play with more flair than they do.

And this is what's at the heart of England's problems. It has taken them a long while to realise that at the top level you need more than talent.

You can't let yourself get out too easily. You've got to have attitude. I don't think they've got it.

Cricket has always been played pretty seriously, but now it's professional, preparation is so much more acute. That is the nature of the game.

In former times, when there wasn't as much cricket played, the players used to have a drink and a smoke, and they didn't think about their physical condition the way today's players do.

When Alan McGilvray retired from the ABC in 1985, he was asked the greatest difference between the game he had played and commentated on pre-war to the game that he was leaving.

"The athleticism of the players," he said. "These

Pigeon Power

HIS AGGRESSION IS ALWAYS THERE, FOR GOOD OR ILL.

There have been times in Glenn McGrath's career when he has allowed his emotions to run away with him, and overreacted when decisions have gone against him. It was evident in the heat of battle with Sachin Tendulkar in the Sydney Test match in 1999 when McGrath was particularly peeved that he didn't get a lbw decision. This isn't unusual in the chronicles of fast bowling, especially where Australian competitors have been involved, but on that occasion there appeared to be more than just glaring going on between the bowler and the batsman. And in the era of the all-pervasive television lens, we can do the lip-reading. McGrath has "white line fever" when things go against him. In more recent times he seems to have come to terms with that and has made a visible effort to pull back. However, that was in England where it didn't matter so much because if a decision went against him he knew it would only be a matter of time before he succeeded. How he'll handle a tight battle with the South Africans remains to be seen.

I've always found him friendly and willing to talk, though there is sometimes a kind of tension about his conversation, a nervous edginess about what he has to say. But he's balanced and articulate.

I can remember interviewing him as a gangly, six-foot-plus youngster when he first came into the NSW side. His nickname then was "Millard", from the brand-name of the caravan he was supposedly living in at the time. Later, as most people know, he acquired the moniker "Pigeon".

Greg Matthews picked him from the start, before he'd even bowled a ball.

"This geezer's going to take 200 Test wickets."

He wasn't quite right — McGrath has taken over 350.

Say so... *"India was pretty bad and pretty embarrassing. I didn't trust my technique, that's what stuffed me. I was always trying to find a different way to play rather than trusting my technique."* **Ricky Ponting**

players are athletes. And this has been brought about by the fact that they are playing for their living."

Has this taken the fun out of it?

I don't think so, not entirely. It's still fun – let's not lose sight of that – but it's not the barrel of laughs it may once have been, when we had those "rest" days.

The seriousness of Australia's aproach was evident in the preparations for the First Test at Edgbaston. I provided this piece for the BBC website at the time:

"We tell stories in order to live. Any Australian perspective on an Ashes series is like the boy's own story of action, daring, celebration, cockiness, disappointment and then, inspiringly, the counterwheeling victory.

"And this team knows all about victories. It is the most victorious Australian team ever, and only a mug would tip against them.

"They are victorious and confident. So confident that they named their team three days before the match – unprecedented.

"The decision to leave Justin Langer out was taken entirely on form. His omission was harsh, but fair.

"No room for sentiment, no blind faith in a player who'd scored the most runs in the record-breaking 16-match sequence, and could be forgiven a cluster of failures in the Test lead-up.

"Ponting's form was compelling, and demanded number-three recognition. He will be Australia's best batsman, and like Bradman, first drop is where the main man bats.

"Martyn has been harshly denied opportunities, appearing only when Ponting or Steve Waugh were injured. The new number six is a more mature, athletic Martyn than the kid on Easy Street in 1993. Like his team-mates, cricket has become a hungry vocation, and second chances are as rare as left-arm West Indian fast bowlers. Many qualities underscore this potent Australian team, but three stand out: confidence, discipline, and taking risks.

"Confidence is not just assertiveness. Plenty of Aussies love to assert themselves without necessarily being confident. They're called brash, arrogant, generally up themselves and lack the record to justify

Aggers Goes Ape

My BBC colleague Jonathan Agnew drove me to the match the day Australia were playing in Bristol. It's a wonderful, historic ground – WG Grace used to play there years ago – elevated and exposed to the elements, and surrounded by a lot of little streets that lead to it.

Jonathan picked me up in his car at the hotel on the morning of the match, and pointed rather proudly to a high-tech gadget in his BMW, a global navigation system with the nickname "Helga". He turned it on, punched in the address, and let it guide him.

Sure enough it did the trick and we got to the turn-off, only to find that the street was closed off. Jonathan played around with the technology, and away we went to find another street. Road block. By the time we got to the third street that was shut off, Jonathan had had enough. He got out of the car, removed the barricade and drove straight up to the gates where, somewhat reluctantly, we were let in.

The Australian team bus had the same problem. It was stuck in a traffic jam that had to be cleared before they could get into the ground.

The author in a seat he has often swapped with the BBC's Jonathan Agnew.

their bluster. This mob have got the record, and that's why they have so much belief, or confidence, in what they are about. And with that confidence the team has developed what Steve Waugh has euphemistically described as mental disintegration.

"It is sledging; subtle sledging, where you address editorial remarks about an opponent to a team-mate, and not to the opponent's face.

"'Plays the short ball well.' Less sarcastically, 'No ******* idea on the short ****.'

"Call it gamesmanship. Call it what you like. It's part of the intimidation package.

"Tendulkar's bat is the ripest riposte to verbal challenges. But he's not playing for England.

"Then there's discipline. It is epitomised by McGrath and Gillespie's swift, siegelike bowling.

"They aim at a back of a length, on and outside the off stump, and create indecision about whether to play or leave the ball. They prefer consistency to variety, sending the ball whacking into Gilchrist's gloves with metronomic regularity.

"Or the example of Steve Waugh's batting. He's one of the small club of class batsmen who knows how to build a Test innings. Most of his contemporaries

---

Say so... "*We've made a conscious decision this series to accept every umpiring decision. We want to be remembered as a really good cricket side, not for the wrong reasons.*" **Steve Waugh**

---

lapse in technique, or concentration, or both.

"They are one-day flirts. Steve is a fundamentalist – watch the ball, play straight, be patient.

"And he's a risk-taker. It is a state of mind made easier by his bowling weaponry, and the sharpest fielding and catching posse around. Brother Mark must be the best catcher in the game.

"He took six in his last Test, and will probably break Mark Taylor's record at Edgbaston.

"This team has the capacity to score 350 runs a day,

Meet the Family

....

THE DAYS WHEN TOURS WERE "BOYS ONLY" ARE PAST.

Given the year-round schedule of cricket, it's not surprising that the pressures of long absence and off-field temptations occasionally create problems for players and their partners. Steve Waugh described the three-month Ashes tour as "just too long". "I think it can be unhealthy for everyone," he said. "People obviously miss their families."

Things are changing, but wives and girlfriends are still not encouraged to be there throughout a tour.

Arrangements could have been made in India, for instance, to accommodate them but I don't think it would have been looked on as the place to go.

In Australia partners are more often around during a series, and in England, New Zealand and the West Indies they come and go a bit.

You often see the wives watching the cricket and going out together. It's not like the old days where being there at all was basically a no-no.

In terms of keeping some balance in your life it's probably important that partners are there at some stage. It's a changed attitude to the old days when a player was just a bloody number and it was a case of "if you don't like it we'll get someone else". The managers are a bit more caring than they used to be, quite apart from the legal issues that might come up.

> "IT'S A CHANGED ATTITUDE TO THE OLD DAYS WHEN A PLAYER WAS JUST A BLOODY NUMBER."

A case in point was when Michael Slater's relationship broke up. Stephanie Slater is a very bubbly character who was Michael's childhood sweetheart before they got married. But it's a harsh call to say that cricket contributed to the breakdown in their relationship. It could have been for any number of reasons.

Most of the relationships around the Australian team seem to be secure, particularly with the guys who have children.

There must be an incredible understanding on the part of their wives for this to continue, but then again the players are very well paid, so it may be worth the sacrifice, I guess. Under contract they're allowed two months off a year.

And the ACB's recent decision to provide an annual paid airfare and accommodation package for players' wives or partners is another healthy outcome of the work done by the Players Association, under Tim May's guidance.

with Gilchrist averaging 47 at seven, the champion plunderer. And they'll often play risky shots to challenge their virtuosity. Gough and Caddick could spoil the party, but as Michael Slater said pre-match: 'If we play to our potential, 5-nil is a real possibility.'"

The rest of the series I heard and saw from home. I'd got back just after the British Lions were beaten by the resilient Wallabies in the deciding Test at the Olympic Stadium. I'd been in England when the Lions had their

All-round good guys

IN THE ERA OF THE SPECIALIST — AS TRUE OF CRICKET
AS OF EVERYWHERE ELSE — THE VALUE OF THE GENUINE
ALL-ROUNDER SHOULDN'T BE UNDERESTIMATED.

The only genuine all-rounder right now is Adam Gilchrist. But he's in a special context, as a wicket-keeper and a frontline batsman, where his batting at No 7 has been one of the reasons Australia have been able to sustain their incredible performance.

The days of the genuine batting/bowling all-rounder seem to be gone in this world of specialists.

Steve Waugh was a real all-rounder in his younger days – he made his name in the '87 World Cup as a bowling all-rounder – but now his focus is concentrated on batting rather than running the risk of another career-threatening injury.

So the other contenders are more likely to be players who have some ambitions in an area other than their specialist skill.

Shane Warne's batting in the lower order at times has been useful.

In the West Indies in '95 and '99 he played some useful innings, not necessarily making big scores but enough to give the innings some substance.

For a bowler like him there's always the worry, especially facing a seriously quick bowler, that you'll get a potentially disastrous rap on the fingers.

Brett Lee has shown a lot of ability with the bat, and as his career develops it could lead towards him becoming a quasi-all-rounder.

Mark Waugh was a promising medium-fast bowler until he had back problems, and he has been versatile enough as a sportsman to be able to adapt his bowling so that he can have impact with his occasional off-spin.

Ricky Ponting's another one who can

First Test win at the 'Gabba, and the story of their supporters at a lively post-match night out had special flavour. Asked by the MC if they would like to see highlights of the First Test, their roar was deafening – until highlights of the First Test from Edgbaston came up on the screen.

In England, Australia retained the Ashes in just 11 days of domination, winning as decisively at Lord's as they did at Edgbaston.

At Trent Bridge a competitive opening day tumbled away into another three-day Australian win, marred by Steve Waugh's calf muscle injury. Waugh's tour appeared to be over, and he would probably go home before the last Test. Ha ha. Which was probably

Adam Gilchrist: there's no one like him.

roll his arm over quite usefully.

And then, believe it or not, there's the outsider's claim from Glenn McGrath. He had an average of 47 in India, which I'm sure he has reminded his team-mates about. And he has certainly come on. Early in his career he was a genuine rabbit – one of those old-fashioned bowlers who came in with the heavy roller, because it was just a question of when they would be leaving again – after the first or second ball.

But McGrath has stuck at it. A combination of embarrassment and pride, and all the encouragement of the team, have made him work almost as hard on his batting as the rest of his game. And it has shown. He has occupied the crease for quite some time on occasions. Steve Waugh can thank him for helping him get to his double-century in Jamaica in 1995 and past the hundred in Calcutta. McGrath was there to see him over the line. He still doesn't look much better than a rabbit, but he can occupy the crease surprisingly.

the reaction at Bankstown, where Steve's bevy of supporters were predicting his return at the Oval.

For four days Australia created a winning position at Headingley, only to lose out on the final day when a combination of the weather, and dramatically, a memorable Mark Butcher century, produced a shock England victory.

The best comment on England's resurrection shuffle came from the studious, sharp-witted Australian writer, Gideon Haigh.

He was sitting quietly in the midst of England's press box celebration, and remarked, "Haven't you heard of the dead cat bounce?"

It's tough on Adam Gilchrist that Australia lost only one Test in a series that was heading towards a whitewash – and it happened to be on his watch.

It would be wrong to be too judgmental given the circumstances of the game. It ran all the way with Australia for four days, and it was only because of the

Say so... *on losing the First Test ...* "*They completely outplayed us. They're a very fine side and we played below par. We were outplayed in all three departments, to be honest.*" **Nasser Hussain**

weather, with Australia pressing hard to win, that England were left with a target. Over 300 is still a pretty healthy one to achieve on the last day.

England played from a position of nothing to lose, Butcher's innings was wonderful, and Australia didn't bowl or field particularly well.

Lee and Gillespie were pretty wild on that day, though Warne bowled well, but on those fast English ground it's hard to stop a batsman scoring boundaries if he gets away from you.

Whether Gilchrist found the task of concentrating on being both wicket-keeper and captain too difficult is something he'd probably deny. However, for people considering the Australian captaincy in the future it will be something to look at.

It was an example perhaps of a wicket-keeper not being in a position to take full control, because of the need for him to concentrate on his specialist role as well as the overall game. If the opposition sense the pressure isn't being sustained, things can go against you. And Headingley was one of the few occasions when the Australians came under pressure.

I'd be reluctant to judge Gilchrist's ability as a captain on the strength of that one day. Who knows what would have happened if Steve Waugh had been there. He might have set just as attacking fields as Gilchrist, also in the expectation that his bowlers would deliver the knockout punches.

Perhaps it underlines the fact that in any sport you should never give a sucker an even break. One thing's

Taking a Pounding

The days of cheap living in England are a fond but very distant memory. At the time I was there the dollar was worth only slightly better than 35 pence – in other words, three to a pound.

Tickets for the matches cost around 60 quid ($A180), and they were all sold out during the tour. Tickets were trading for some amazing prices. I heard that there were scalpers at Lord's selling them for 1000 pounds each. They were very scarce. An Australia v England Test match is a major event and the support was certainly there for it.

At least I was lucky enough not to have to buy my own tickets. The expense of being in England was enough. Filling the car with petrol cost the same as here, except that it was 80-odd *pence* per litre, not *cents*. So it was between two-and-a-half and three times dearer. It cost me over a hundred dollars to fill it up.

I got to the point where I stopped making the calculation, otherwise I would have lost my sanity.

I had a simple dinner in St Johns Wood one night with Peter Baxter, the long-time producer of BBC cricket – just some pasta and a bottle of wine – and it set me back the best part of 100 pounds.

It would have been fine if the total had been dollars, but it was actually about $A290 when the credit card bill landed.

Say so... "*We made a pact that we were going to play very good, disciplined cricket. Being sharp and hungry was what it was all about. Once you do that you get on a bit of a roll.*" **Steve Waugh**

sure, it was a great motivation for Steve to come back after his calf-muscle injury, to play and bat in the last Test, as he did, on one leg.

The person who deserves the greatest credit is Errol Alcott, the team's physiotherapist. In his capable hands, Steve went from considering going home because the injury looked to be so serious to making an amazing recovery. His determination was fired by the prospect of a match that would be a defining moment in his career: the last time he'd play a Test match in England. It's pretty emotional to play at the Oval and to win.

He just wanted to be there. It was yet another example of his famous line: "I'm never satisfied." He'd have needed to have calf injuries to both legs to have been out of the side.

Australia only lost four wickets in the last Test and won by an innings. Forget captaincy issues, it was an emphatic reminder of the gap between the two teams.

And so Steve Waugh returned, as expected at Bankstown, from injury, and although he was something of a one-legged wonder, that was all he needed to embarrass England. His 27th Test century ensured Australia's mammoth total of 641.

England took some prising out; the clincher came in their second innings, after following on, when McGrath produced a snorter that Trescothick could only instinctively jab at, sending a gentle catch back to the bowler.

McGrath and Warne shared the spoils, wearing England down again to complete an innings win.

Australia finished the series as they had begun, and

re-emphasised why they are the best in world cricket.

To win at the Oval, with a 4-1 wash-up in the Ashes series, was a rewarding moment for Steve Waugh.

The only thing that would have gratified him even more would have been for someone from Lord's to turn up at the end of match and, instead of giving him the beautiful Waterford crystal replica of the Ashes, to give him the real thing.

That would have been the perfect finish to the series. It didn't happen, though we all know it should have. And it won't happen.

It's a hopelessly inadequate response from England. There's no reason for those Ashes to stay locked up in the museum at Lord's. To say they're too unsafe to be moved around is just camouflage.

There are always ways. They were brought here in 1988 for the Bicentennial Test match between Australia and England.

The fact is the Ashes should be in Australia. It would give England a reason to try to win them back.

It's Academic

It was announced that England have decided to employ Rod Marsh, not one of their own, to run their cricket academy. If they asked anyone in Australia they'd probably hear the view that the academy here has run its course. Most of the state associations are doing their own thing now.

The Australian Cricket Academy certainly had its place in its time, but a combination of changing attitudes, logistics and the fact that maybe Rod Marsh's ideas are becoming outmoded all means that the academy is less important than people think.

For England it's a band-aid approach. Their real problem is the inadequacy of the county championship to provide enough hard competition.

It's a structural issue. But there are too many vested interests, too little will to change.

It's like so many other things in England. People love to take a cheap weekend trip to Prague, for instance, or some other wonderful destination in Europe, but on the other hand the last thing they want to do is be part of Europe. They're living in the past. It really is an extraordinary country.

Looking Back

Cricket lovers have been living in
interesting times. Whatever the future
holds, let's give credit to
Steve Waugh and his team for playing
the most attractive cricket imaginable.

One of my favourite cricket books is Arthur Mailey's "10 for 66 and All That", published in 1958. It's full of thoughtful and amusing observations, anecdotes about his life, and about the game that took him far from his humble upbringing.

Mailey bowled leg spinners and wrong 'uns in another golden era of Australian cricket, the 1920s, when Australia beat England in three consecutive series.

Mailey's autobiography includes an illusory, dream meeting between Trumper and Bradman over dinner at Mailey's shack at Burraneeer Bay, south of Sydney. Mailey imaginatively observed; "Bradman's eyes and the curl of his lips gave no indication of what he was really thinking. He might have been facing a Larwood on a lively pitch, a gang of cricket reporters – or contemplating the ups and downs of the stock exchange. Trumper's face on the other hand, fully illustrated his thoughts."

The conversation, recalling Bradman's sharp mind and Trumper's casual nonchalance, moved on to the subject of batting on a "sticky wicket". The modern equivalent, if there is one with pitches fully covered for almost half a century now, would probably be a dry, cobra-spitting turner, a bit like the worst features of the pitch used for the First Test at Mumbai in 2001.

Trumper, in this superbly crafted fictional account, told Bradman that you could never learn to bat on a sticky by playing on it. He learnt by asking the SCG curator to water one end of a practice pitch before the other players arrived, so that he could develop a "sticky wicket" technique. He was considered by his contemporaries to be masterly on a "sticky".

Today the thought of batting on anything as treacherous as a soft, rain-affected pitch would be tantamount to suggesting that players sleep in one-star hotels on tour, and fly down the back of a plane.

So it was fascinating to watch that practice session in Chennai before the Third Test this year when Steve Waugh deliberately roughed up an area outside the off stump, creating an uneven patch that mirrored the likely match conditions he would encounter against the

The Australian players celebrate the retention of the Ashes after victory in the Third Test at Trent Bridge, in a series they won 4-1.

skilful Harbhajan Singh. In another net Justin Langer, who practises as assiduously as Geoffrey Boycott used to, observed his captain's innovative routine, and followed suit. Langer's lingering sessions, before, during, after play had tended to be repetitive. He was perpetually forward or back to throwdowns, mainly from the indefatigable coach John Buchanan.

Hard work usually brings a reward, but when you're constantly being befuddled by a quality off-spinner, the need to practise against something similar seems at least practical. Old masters of playing spin, such as Harvey, Redpath and Walters would have been sharper on their feet than most of today's stars, but the bowling was probably more tantalising than dartlike.

Langer's sweeping methods certainly weren't as effective as Hayden's, who had a better judgment of length, and for a tall, heavy-footed bludgeoner, he was deceptively quick to pounce. Alas for Waugh, the practice didn't prevent his dismissal from a million-to-one aberration, when he was out, handled the ball.

Mailey rounds out his zestful book with a chapter entitled, "Cricket – Its Joy and Its Future".

Remember he was writing in 1958, at a time when television coverage in Australia was in its infancy.

He lamented the potential loss of gate money, assuming fans would prefer an armchair to an uncomfortable seat on the Hill or in the grandstand. Presciently he wrote, "It is quite possible that powerful television corporations will buy up Test teams lock, stock and barrel." It took another 20 years for Mailey's prophecy to come true, when Kerry Packer contracted the best players to his televised World Series.

In 1976 Packer met with the Australian Cricket Board to discuss an exclusive three-year deal, but the Board had already shaken hands with the ABC for $210,000 over the next three years. Packer then offered $1.5 million for three years when the ABC's contract expired, if they signed immediately. The Board said come back in three years time. Packer set about creating his own rival operation. As related elsewhere in this book, I well remember the day in 1977 when Packer held a press conference to announce the birth of WSC. Smoke, and steam, rose from behind the desk, as he denounced those who couldn't see the WSC's credibility.

Packer really had no interest in running cricket, but a combination of satisfying Australian content rules, a surge in the popularity of televised sport with the introduction of colour television in 1973, and players who were disgruntled about pay and the feudal administration of cricket, played easily into his hands. When peace was eventually negotiated between WSC and the ACB in 1978, Packer got what he wanted: the goldmine of exclusive television coverage, and the bonus of marketing and promotional rights.

From the comfort of a 2001 armchair, or the commentary box, Australian cricket looks healthy, indeed prosperous. And for much of that prosperity the game's followers can thank Kerry Packer. This unloved entrepreneur placed a large firecracker under the incestuous honoraries at the ACB, and there is no doubt that his pyjama game revitalised interest in cricket, and introduced it to a new audience. The board still sat back and got fat on the easy money from its most generous sponsor, Benson and Hedges, failing to give enough of the proceeds from that largesse and television rights to the players.

More recently the development of a strong players' association has given the sportsmen who ensure that the grounds swell for big matches, a generous reward for their efforts. In that sense the ACB's administration under Malcolm Speed and Denis Rogers stewardship has made excellent advances, bringing together the needs of sponsors, media and the players for the long-term benefit of the game and its followers.

As you read these closing words, the news of a high honour for Steve Waugh is probably about. He deserves it, and so does his team, for bringing so much pleasure to all of us with the most attractive cricket imaginable.

Honours have their place but, for the last word, this is from that wonderful cricketer and cartoonist, Arthur Mailey: "A bee is not expected to put honey back into the flower. But she must not harm the flower."

From the comfort of a 2001 armchair, or the commentary box, Australian cricket looks healthy, indeed prosperous.

Index